For

....

From

....

Date

....

Fill My Cup, Lord

DONNA K. MALTESE

Fill My Cup, Lord

Devotions and Prayers for a Blessed Life

BARBOUR
PUBLISHING

Print ISBN 979-8-89151-164-4

Published by Barbour Publishing, Inc., 1810 Barbour Drive, Uhrichsville, Ohio 44683, www.barbourbooks.com

Our mission is to inspire the world with the life-changing message of the Bible.

ecpa Member of the Evangelical Christian Publishers Association

Printed in China.

Introduction

God can pour on the blessings in astonishing ways so that you're ready for anything and everything, more than just ready to do what needs to be done. As one psalmist puts it, He throws caution to the winds, giving to the needy in reckless abandon. His right-living, right-giving ways never run out, never wear out. This most generous God who gives seed to the farmer that becomes bread for your meals is more than extravagant with you.

2 CORINTHIANS 9:8–10 MSG

Every day God gifts us with His wonders, blessings, peace, and promises. Yet too often we spend our time focused on the ugliness of the world, seeming "curses," criticisms of others, and broken promises. But that is *not* how God wants His people to live.

The devotions that follow can help you fix your mind on things worthy of your thoughts. Instead of shuffling "along, eyes to the ground, absorbed with the things right in front of you," you will be inspired to "look up, and be alert to what is going on around Christ—that's where the action is. See things from *his* perspective" (Colossians 3:2 MSG). May you be blessed as you do so.

The Genesis of Blessings

God blessed them. And God said to them, "Be fruitful and multiply and fill the earth and subdue it, and have dominion over the fish of the sea and over the birds of the heavens and over every living thing that moves on the earth."

Genesis 1:28 ESV

God has been blessing His creation from the very beginning of time. His first blessing was to the sea creatures that swarmed the waters and the birds that flew above the earth. He instructed them to be fruitful, multiply, and fill their domains (Genesis 1:22).

On the sixth day, God made earthly beasts—livestock and wild animals. Then He said, "Let Us [Father, Son, and Holy Spirit] make mankind in Our image, after Our likeness, and let them have complete authority over the fish of the sea, the birds of the air, the [tame] beasts, and over all of the earth, and over everything that creeps upon the earth" (Genesis 1:26 AMPC). So God made man and woman in His image. Afterward, when He blessed the newly created Adam and Eve, He told them not just to be fruitful and multiply but to *subdue* the earth, to rule over it and its creatures!

Along with that blessing, God told the humans that every plant and tree He created were to be food for them and all the other creatures He'd formed. In other words, God's initial blessing to Adam and Eve came with provisions (food) for them, ones that would help them be fruitful and multiply!

The point is, if God blesses you, He will also *provide* for you, giving you everything you need to experience that blessing. And once blessed, you are always blessed.

Yet if humans are to continue to be blessed by God, we also need to adhere to His instructions. For example, trees, plants, and animals have been put under our care. If we are lax in our responsibility, if we neglect our caretaking obligations, we will have difficulty being fruitful and multiplying. And God's initial provisions will dry up.

God has lovingly blessed us. But experiencing that blessing is contingent on abiding by His instructions for what we are to do—what we *need* to do—to realize that blessing.

Taking God's start-up blessing for granted would spell disaster. So, woman, prayerfully consider what God may be calling you to, what part He may have you play in taking care of Earth's environs and inhabitants, whether they be animal, human, vegetable, or mineral. Then walk where He leads, doing your part to follow His commands and praising Him for His blessing upon you.

Lord, thank You for Your blessing and Your provision. Help me understand that along with Your blessings come responsibilities. Show me what You would have me do and where You would have me go to fulfill them. Amen.

The Blessing of Rest

On the seventh day God finished his work that he had done, and he rested on the seventh day from all his work that he had done. So God blessed the seventh day and made it holy, because on it God rested from all his work that he had done in creation.

GENESIS 2:2–3 ESV

Just as a parent aims to set an example for her children, Father God set an example for His own kids. After God spent six days creating all that we can still see, touch, taste, hear, and feel on, in, under, and above our terrestrial sphere, He rested on the seventh day.

Because God rested on that day, He blessed it. Made it holy. Knowing the importance of the seventh-day rest, God commanded us to follow His example, saying, "Remember the Sabbath day, to keep it holy. Six days you shall labor, and do all your work, but the seventh day is a Sabbath to the LORD your God" (Exodus 20:8–10 ESV).

Not only were God's people to rest on the Sabbath, but so were their kids, servants, livestock, and foreign visitors. Then He gives them the reason: "For in six days the LORD made heaven and earth, the sea, and all that is in them, and rested on the seventh day. Therefore the LORD blessed the Sabbath day and made it holy" (Exodus 20:11 ESV).

This commandment (along with the other nine) was reiterated forty years later by Moses in Deuteronomy 5:12–14 with one slight variation—the reason *why* the people were to rest on the Sabbath: "You shall remember that you were a slave in the land of Egypt, and the LORD your God brought you out from there with a mighty hand and an outstretched arm. Therefore the LORD your God commanded you to keep the Sabbath day" (Deuteronomy 5:15 ESV).

Today some Christian denominations maintain that it's necessary to observe the Sabbath to be saved. Others say that since we are no longer living under the law as the Jews did, the Sabbath need not be observed—even though both Christ and the apostles kept the Sabbath. There are even questions about which day is technically considered the Sabbath day.

So what's a good Christian woman to do? Find some time—whether it be every day or one entire day a week or both—to be with God. To focus on Him. To praise and worship Him. And, most of all, to rest in Him. When you do so, you'll not only be pleasing God but also be getting the rest you need to serve Him. What a blessing!

Lord, thank You for giving me an excuse to rest from my labors and set aside a special time and day just for You. Help me find a way to keep a time of Sabbath so that I can restore and refresh myself in You. In Jesus' name, amen.

Blessed in So Many Words

What time I am afraid, I will have confidence in and put my trust and reliance in You. By [the help of] God I will praise His word; on God I lean, rely, and confidently put my trust; I will not fear. What can man, who is flesh, do to me?

Psalm 56:3–4 AMPC

The book of Psalms is filled with wonderful imagery and the recorded thoughts of God's people. It helps us to see that thousands of years ago, believers had the same burdens and blessings we have today. The psalmists give us words we can use to pray back to God. They help us to understand we aren't the first to doubt, fear, cry, laugh, celebrate, praise, ponder, and shake our heads in bewilderment. In the chapters of Psalms, we also find words that can become the building blocks of our faith.

Psalm 56 was written by David. It's a record of his thoughts when the Philistines had seized him in Gath (1 Samuel 21:10–15). In his escape from King Saul, David ran to King Achish of Gath, a Philistine city. But when Achish's servants reminded him of how many Philistines David had killed (tens of thousands), David became frightened. So he pretended to be insane, drooling and scribbling nonsense on doors. So Achish allowed David to leave Gath and seek refuge elsewhere.

Although we may not be insane, we can still examine, learn from, and use this psalm in a general way, for its words do not link it to the specific event David experienced. And even though the word *blessing* is not used once in Psalm 56, it can be found *behind* the recorded words.

The psalmist makes it clear he's tired of being trampled by attackers and enemies. Yet when he is assaulted, when he is afraid, he puts his trust in God. He asks, "What can flesh do to me?" (verse 4 ESV).

All day long people are against the psalmist. Stalking him. Ready to take his life. But he knows that God is keeping track of all the sleepless nights he's had. That God counts each of his tears and puts them in a bottle, records them in His book. The psalmist knows, as do each of us, that "God is on my side" (verse 9 MSG).

When we realize God is with us, when we put all our trust in Him, we too can say, "God, you did everything you promised, and I'm thanking you with all my heart. You pulled me from the brink of death. . . . Now I stroll at leisure with God in the sunlit fields of life" (verses 12–13 MSG). What a blessing—to know God is with us, we can trust Him, and He is true to His promises!

I want to have the same mindset as David in this psalm, Lord. Help me get there from here. Remind me every moment that You are with me, for me, and watching over me. Amen.

The Lord's Reward

Boaz replied to her, "All that you have done for your mother-in-law after the death of your husband has been fully reported to me. . . . May the Lord *reward your work, and your wages be full from the* Lord*, the God of Israel, under whose wings you have come to seek refuge."*

RUTH 2:11–12 NASB

Have you ever experienced a time—whether it be a moment, hour, day, week, or year—when everything you touched, said, attempted, or did had good if not remarkable results? Ever wondered why that day or project or task turned out so well? Perhaps it was because God was rewarding you for your attitude, kindness, commitment, faith, or stubborn perseverance. That's what He did for Ruth—one of only two women (the other being Esther) who had a book of the Bible named after her.

Ruth's story begins with Naomi's. Naomi and her husband, Elimelech, along with their two sons, left Bethlehem during a famine. They landed in Moab. There their sons—Mahlon and Chilion—each married a Moabitess, one named Ruth and the other Orpah. And there all three men eventually died, leaving first Naomi and then her two daughters-in-law as widows.

When Naomi found out that the famine in Judah had ended, she decided to say goodbye to her daughters-in-law and walk back to Bethlehem. But Ruth insisted on going with her, saying, "Do not urge me to leave you or turn back from following you; for where you go, I will go, and where you lodge,

I will lodge. Your people shall be my people, and your God, my God" (Ruth 1:16 NASB).

Then, once in Bethlehem, Ruth followed Naomi's advice to "go to the field and glean among the ears of grain" (Ruth 2:2 NASB) in the field of Boaz, a rich relative of Elimelech. When Boaz was told Ruth was in his fields, gleaning grain, he spoke with her, telling her he'd heard about all she'd done for her mother-in-law, Naomi. How she left her own home and family to come to a strange land and live among strangers. Then he blessed her, saying, "May the LORD reward your work, and your wages be full from the LORD. . .under whose wings you have come to seek refuge" (2:12 NASB).

Woman of God, your Lord sees what you're doing. He knows what help you have given others. He knows how you have sought refuge under His wings. And He wants you to know that for all you selflessly do, He will reward you—if not here on earth, then in heaven above.

Lord, I thank You for being such a generous God. Help me keep Your generosity in mind when I see someone who needs my support, my strength, my home, and my heart. Help me do what You would have me do. Amen.

God of Second Chances

God blessed Noah and his sons and said to them,
"Be fruitful and multiply, and fill the earth."
GENESIS 9:1 NASB

God had created Adam and Eve. All was good until they ate the forbidden fruit and were banned from the Garden of Eden. Then they had two sons, Cain and Abel. And that was great, until Cain killed Abel. After God banished a forever-marked Cain, Eve had another son, Seth. It's a wonder God didn't give up on this creation idea. But He stuck with it as the humans continued to procreate, just as He'd commanded (be fruitful and multiply).

Then one day God looked down on His creation and saw how corrupt humankind had become. Things had degenerated so quickly and so thoroughly that God "was sorry that He had made man on the earth, and He was grieved in His heart" (Genesis 6:6 NASB). He was ready to obliterate the entirety of His creation! But then a "but" arrives on the scene in the form of Noah: "*But* Noah found favor in the eyes of the LORD" (Genesis 6:8 NASB, emphasis added).

God saw a ray of hope in Noah—the only righteous person left on earth. And to Noah God gave the command to build an ark. And "by faith Noah, being warned by God about things not yet seen, in reverence prepared an ark for the salvation of his household, by which he condemned the world, and became an heir of the righteousness which is according to faith" (Hebrews 11:7 NASB).

God's plan worked. Noah and his wife, along with his three sons and their wives, as well as the animals on the ark, escaped the floodwaters. All the bad stuff was washed away. It was a fresh start for humankind.

God then blessed Noah and his sons, telling them to repopulate the earth. God even made a new covenant with Noah, vowing never again to wipe out humankind with a flood. The Lord even gave Noah a sign as a reminder of His promise—the rainbow.

After receiving God's blessing and promise, Noah planted a vineyard, got drunk, and wound up naked in his tent, sleeping off the effects of his drinking binge. Two out of three sons respectfully covered up their father's nakedness.

The account of Noah's adventures reminds us of God's absolute power to destroy and to rebuild. It shows He loves us so much He's willing to continually forgive us, redeem us, help us find a new way of living, doing, and being. The story also reveals that even the most righteous of men and women can sometimes disappoint themselves, God, and others. But if we stumble—and we will—we can be sure our loving God, through His mercy and grace, will give us a second chance.

God of mercy and grace, thank You for looking after me. For being a God of second chances. Amen.

Stepping Out Steeped in Faith

"Go from your country and your kindred and your father's house to the land that I will show you. And I will make of you a great nation, and I will bless you and make your name great, so that you will be a blessing. I will bless those who bless you, and him who dishonors you I will curse, and in you all the families of the earth shall be blessed."

GENESIS 12:1–3 ESV

God has designed things so that believers will not just be blessed by Him but become a blessing themselves! He has also arranged things so that those who bless believers will be blessed by Him!

It all began with Abraham. But before he could be blessed, be a blessing, and be an avenue through which others would be blessed, Abraham needed to have enough faith in God to say yes to His call, to do what God wanted him to do, and to go to a place he had never seen and dwell there, living like a stranger.

Yet that's just what Abraham did. For he knew early on that "without faith it is impossible to please and be satisfactory to Him. For whoever would come near to God must [necessarily] believe that God exists and that He is the rewarder of those who earnestly and diligently seek Him [out]" (Hebrews 11:6 AMPC). And Abraham believed: "He put his trust in God. This made Abraham right with God" (Galatians 3:6 NLV).

God wants *you* to trust Him totally too. To walk where He tells you to walk. And to do it one step at a time—without knowing what's in front of you. That truly is blind faith.

Yet Abraham wasn't without troubles, obstacles he had to overcome on his trek with God. He had to trust that God had only good in mind for him. He needed to look beyond what he could see to what God Himself sees.

Today, tune in to the Lord. Ask Him what He sees for you. Apply to Him for the faith you may need to walk the pathway He is drawing you to, knowing faith is what you will need to complete the journey. Get up close to the Lord, knowing He will reward you if you trust Him and keep on seeking Him. Then you too will be blessed in being right with God!

Lord, give me the faith I need to walk the way You would have me walk, to go where You would have me go, to do what You would have me do. Keep holding my hand the whole way as You bless me and make me a blessing to others. In Jesus' name, amen.

The God Who Sees

The angel of the LORD found her. . . . And he said, "Hagar, servant of Sarai, where have you come from and where are you going?" She said, "I am fleeing from my mistress Sarai." The angel of the LORD said to her, "Return to your mistress and submit to her."

GENESIS 16:7–9 ESV

It's one thing to be told God is going to bless you. It's another thing entirely to believe that blessing will ultimately come to fruition. Yet that's exactly what God wants you to do. For it's your belief that will bring the blessing into being.

Consider Sarah. God had told her husband, Abraham, that He was going to bless him with countless descendants (Genesis 15:5). Abraham believed the Lord, and "that made him right with God" (Genesis 15:6 NLV). But as the years went by, Sarah remained barren. Impatient, she decided to take matters into her own hands so that she and Abraham could realize God's promised blessing.

Disbelieving God is where God's children trip up. That's when unforeseen and unwanted consequences come into play.

Because Sarah grew impatient, she gave her maid Hagar to her husband, Abraham. If Hagar got pregnant, she would be giving birth to a child on Sarah's behalf. But that wasn't what God had in mind. He wanted to see Sarah trusting Him enough to leave things in His hands.

Women like to fix situations. They want to make things right. Although their intentions might be good, the consequences can be disastrous.

Sarah did give her maid to Abraham. Hagar did get pregnant. But when she began to show, she lorded her condition over Sarah, perhaps even taunting her barrenness. Relations kept deteriorating until, with Abraham's do-whatever-you-want-to-do-with-your-servant consent, Sarah started treating Hagar so harshly that Hagar ran away.

But God saw. God always sees. The angel of the Lord "found" Hagar near a spring in the wilderness on the road to Shur. The angel told Hagar that running away from her mistress was no solution. Instead she was to go back. To submit to Sarah. In return, God would bless her with so many offspring that she herself would not be able to count them all. "So she called the name of the LORD who spoke to her, 'You are a God of seeing,' for she said, 'Truly here I have seen him who looks after me'" (Genesis 16:13 ESV).

Whatever blessing you're waiting for is already in God's hands. But it won't be delivered until everything is ready. Yet it's all in God's timing—not yours. For He alone knows the future.

God has promised you a blessing. But it's His role to deliver it, to bring it to fruition. The only part you have to play is to continue to obey God, to trust in His timing, and to believe He will bring it to pass.

Help me, Lord, to be patient and obedient and to continue to trust in You as I await Your blessings. Amen.

Nothing Too Hard for God

"Is anything too hard for the Lord?"
Genesis 18:14 ESV

Depending on each woman's life experience, she might consider some blessings promised by God to be impossible of fulfillment. Sarah did.

One day, three men stopped in to see Abraham when he was sitting at the door of his tent on a very hot day. One of them happened to be the Lord. Abraham and Sarah rushed to feed the trio. While Abraham stood by them as they ate, they asked where Sarah was.

Abraham told them she was in the tent. That's when the Lord told the elderly Abraham that at the same time next year, Sarah would have a son.

Sarah, eavesdropping from just inside the tent entrance, began laughing. After all, she was way past childbearing age. So she said to herself, "Yeah. Right. As if an old woman like me has a chance of getting pregnant by an old man at this stage of our lives."

God, overhearing Sarah's laughter and remark, asked Abraham, "Why did Sarah laugh and say, 'How can I give birth to a child when I am so old?' Is anything too hard for the Lord? I will return to you at this time next year, and Sarah will have a son" (Genesis 18:13–14 NLV).

Amazingly enough, on top of her doubting God's promise, Sarah responded to God with an actual lie! "Sarah said, 'I did not laugh,' because she was afraid. And He said, 'No, but you did laugh'" (Genesis 18:15 NLV).

It makes one stop and think about how gentle, patient, and long-suffering our Lord is. How He is constantly coming through on doing the impossible in our lives—in spite of our lack of faith in His provision and promises. God continues to come after us and bless us day after day—regardless of what doubts we may be harboring in our heart of hearts, what snickers we may be hiding behind our hands, what lessons we continue to miss, and what faults we exhibit time and time again.

Today, consider which promise of God you would like to see fulfilled in your life, no matter how seemingly impossible you may believe it to be. Pray to God, asking His take on the situation. Then leave all things in His hands, knowing that in His own time and way, He will turn what seems impossible into a reality before your very eyes!

You, Lord, are always doing the impossible. Yet You have promised us certain blessings. So I come before You today, Lord, asking You to give me the faith and trust I need to believe in Your promises. Then help me leave all these things in Your hands, knowing You will always find a way to make what I think impossible, possible! Amen.

Leaving the Past Behind

"Escape for your life! Do not look behind you, and do not stay anywhere in the valley." . . . But his wife, from behind him, looked back, and she became a pillar of salt.

GENESIS 19:17, 26 NASB

God has such compassion, providing us with myriads of opportunities to make the right choice, follow His guidance, put our trust in Him. But we are a stubborn people who sometimes get so stuck in the past, glorifying what once was, that we miss the opportunities of new beginnings, often to our detriment. Ever since the Fall, we've had it in our heads that we know what's best. We believe we are smarter or have more insight than the one who created us! We "the created" assume we have a better handle on what to do in this world than the one who created us! The situation is almost comical. Yet it can also be quite deadly.

Case in point: Lot's wife. When God sent angels into her hometown of Sodom, the plan was for them to get Lot's family out before the fire and brimstone hit. The angels arrived the night before the city's day of reckoning. They told Lot exactly what was going to happen, saying, "If you have any more family members, you're going to want to warn them, to get them out of here before we destroy this sin-filled city at God's direction."

So Lot went out and told his sons-in-law. But they thought he was joking. At dawn, the angels pushed Lot, his two daughters, and his wife out the door. Yet even Lot was dragging his feet. Obviously, things weren't going according to what he'd planned for himself and his family. But the angels insisted they flee, saying, "Now run for your life! Don't look back! Don't stop anywhere on the plain—run for the hills or you'll be swept away" (Genesis 19:17 MSG).

In the end, Lot and his daughters made it out. But Lot's wife got stuck where she stood, looking back at what she'd had and what would soon be lost. What Mrs. Lot didn't understand is that the past is just that: past. There is no going back—especially if God wants you to move forward.

If God takes you away from the home you once knew, the job you once loved, or the status you once enjoyed, trust that He has a better plan for you. That better days lie ahead. And don't worry. God's got this. God's got you.

Lord, help me believe that what You say is true. Help me trust that You know what's best for me. Help me not to look back at what once was but to move forward with You in a new tomorrow. In Jesus' name, amen.

Eyes and Ears Opened

The angel of God called to Hagar from heaven, and said, "Why are you so troubled, Hagar? Do not be afraid. For God has heard the cry of the boy. Get up. Lift up the boy and hold him by the hand. For I will make a great nation of him." Then God opened Hagar's eyes. And she saw a well of water.

GENESIS 21:17–19 NLV

Sarah's son, Isaac, had grown and was now weaned. So Abraham held a big dinner party to celebrate. At that party, Sarah saw Abraham and Hagar's son, Ishmael, mocking his little half brother, Isaac. So Sarah told Abraham to drive Hagar and Ishmael away.

The heart of Abraham, a father who obviously loved his son and perhaps held some affection for Hagar, was torn up at Sarah's demand. But God told him not to worry but to abide by Sarah's demand. God would bless Ishmael as well as Isaac. After all, they were both from the seed of His friend Abraham.

So Abraham got up early, gave Hagar some provisions, and sent her away with Ishmael. Hagar wandered around aimlessly, soon losing her way in the wilderness. When the pair ran out of water, Hagar made the boy lie beneath a shrub. Then, not wanting to watch her son die, she moved some distance away.

The boy must have been crying because the Bible says God heard Ishmael's voice. So the angel of God called out to Hagar from heaven, saying, "Fear not, for God has heard the voice of the boy where he is" (Genesis 21:17 ESV). Then came a promise by God that He would make Ishmael a great nation.

It was then, at that moment, that God provided exactly what Hagar and her son needed at that time. He opened up Hagar's eyes. Then she saw the well of water, filled their empty water bottle, and gave the boy a drink. The chapter ends with God being with Ishmael as he grew. Ishmael lived in the wilderness, became an expert archer, married a woman from Egypt, and went on to have twelve sons of his own, just as his half brother, Isaac, did.

Woman, God sees what's happening in your world, just as He saw what was happening in Hagar's. He knows exactly what you need in the moment, not just physically but spiritually, emotionally, financially, and mentally. He knows that along with the basics—food, water, shelter, and clothing—you need a word of hope for what is to come. Your job is merely to turn to God, explain your story, obey His direction, and watch Him make things right—in heaven and on earth.

Lord, thank You for always being there, for hearing my cry, seeing my situation, and knowing and providing just what I need exactly when I need it. It is You to whom I pray and bring my praise. Amen.

The Lord Will Provide

Abraham raised his eyes and looked, and behold, behind him a ram caught in the thicket by his horns; and Abraham went and took the ram and offered him up for a burnt offering in the place of his son. Abraham called the name of that place The Lord Will Provide.

GENESIS 22:13–14 NASB

Every now and then, schoolteachers give tests to see where students are, how much they've learned, and where they might be falling short in knowledge. God does the same sort of thing with His own students. Every now and then, He gives a sort of life test. He too wants to see where His people are, how much they've learned, and where they might need more lessons.

Such was the case with Abraham, an old man who had fathered two sons. The oldest, Ishmael, was recently sent away. And now God tells Abraham, "Take now your son, your only son, whom you love, Isaac, and go to the land of Moriah, and offer him there as a burnt offering" (Genesis 22:2 NASB).

There's no hint that Abraham rebelled at or was worried about this command. He simply got up early the next day, saddled his donkey, took two young men and his son Isaac, split some wood for the offering fire, and went to Moriah. Once there he told the two servants to wait with the donkey while he and Isaac went to worship God. Once at the site to which God had directed him, Abraham put the wood on the shoulders of Isaac and held the fire in his own hand, along with the knife. The two walked to the sacrifice site.

That's when Isaac noted they had everything but the offering. Isaac said, "'Where is the lamb for the burnt offering?' Abraham said, 'God will provide for Himself the lamb'" (Genesis 22:7–8 NASB).

When they got to the sacrifice site, Abraham built the altar and arranged the offering. Just as he was about to kill his son, an angel of the Lord stayed his hand, telling him, "Now I know that you fear God, since you have not withheld your son, your only son, from Me" (Genesis 22:12 NASB). That's when Abraham saw a ram caught in a thicket and offered the animal in the place of his son. Abraham then named the place "The Lord Will Provide."

Perhaps you know a place where God brought you. A place where God provided just what you needed just in time. It was then you suddenly realized He had, has, and continues to have for you a blessing with an unending source of provision.

Never doubt God's passion for providing just what you need—every day and in every way. Nothing more and nothing less. God has you covered.

Thank You, Lord, for covering me in every situation. With You in my life, I need never fear but simply act on what You require, knowing You'll be sure to bless me. Amen.

A Servant's Journey: A Master's Faith

The Lord, the God of heaven. . .will send His Angel before you, and you will take a wife from there for my son.
GENESIS 24:7 AMPC

When someone is strong in faith, accepts God's statements as truth, and lives a life reflecting his beliefs, that person's faith cannot but affect markedly the lives of those around him. Such was the case with Abraham and his servant.

Abraham was so obedient and faithful to God that he was referred to as God's friend by people (2 Chronicles 20:7; James 2:23) and by God Himself (Isaiah 41:8). And it is this same close friend, follower of God, and widower, a man whom the "LORD had blessed. . .in every way" (Genesis 24:1 NASB), who, in his very old age, asks his oldest and most faithful servant to find a bride for his son Isaac.

The bride the servant is to seek *must* be from Abraham's family back in the city of Nahor. After defining the parameters of the bride-seeking endeavor, Abraham blesses his servant, saying, "The LORD, the God of heaven. . .will send His angel before you, and you will take a wife for my son from there" (Genesis 24:7 NASB).

When was the last time you were blessed with such a statement before what would prove to be a particularly challenging task? When was the last time *you* made such a statement to another person before he or she set off to undertake an arduous assignment?

Abraham was not just a man of great faith—he was also amazingly obedient to his Lord. For the two—faith and obedience—go hand in hand. A great faith leads you to obedient behavior.

The first person in the Bible to say that God can and will send an angel to go before another person is God's friend Abraham (a comment that is later repeated by Abraham's servant in Genesis 24:40). The only other individual who says this is God Himself (Exodus 23:20; 32:34; 33:2)!

When you are unsure of your footing, uncertain of how a situation is going to turn out, when you feel like the task before you is perhaps more than you can handle, remember God's friend Abraham and God Himself. Make it a certainty in your own mind that because you walk in faith and obedience, "the Lord, the God of heaven. . .will send His Angel before you." That's a promise, a certainty that will give you the confidence to move forward and to do so in God's way.

Help me, Lord, to remember that You are always with me. Remind me that no matter where I go, You have already sent Your angel ahead to mark out my path. For this, I praise You! In Jesus' name, amen.

The Servant's Prayer

O Lord, God of my master Abraham, I pray You,
cause me to meet with good success today,
and show kindness to my master Abraham.
GENESIS 24:12 AMPC

Once you've decided you are going to make a move in a certain direction, perhaps step out of your comfort zone and into a new venture, it's great to begin with a blessing from someone of faith. But the first and best thing you can do for yourself is begin with prayer—if you want to meet with success in your endeavors.

Abraham's servant, knowing God would send His angel ahead of him as he began his trek to find a bride for Isaac, took ten camels and assorted goods from his master and traveled to Nahor. He stopped outside the city at the well where women would come to draw water in the evening hours. It was there Abraham's servant made his camels kneel before he began to pray.

This servant's actions are a reminder that before entering into prayer, all distractions and obligations must be set aside. For then the prayer is sure to come from one's heart of hearts.

And so the servant starts to pray, asking for success in his mission. He explains where he is and why, asking God to see him and his circumstances. He asks God for guidance, to demonstrate for him which woman is the one *God* has appointed for Isaac.

Prayers in which the control of the situation and the answer to the prayer itself are seen as in God's hands are the ones that are answered. Here the petitioner is asking for God to make things clear, knowing that the situation, the answer, and the lives of others are to be directed by God, not by the person making the prayer.

As it turns out, God answers the servant's prayer and does so "before he had finished speaking" (Genesis 24:15 AMPC)! The girl whom God clearly showed as being "the one" for Isaac turned out to be from Abraham's family! When the servant realized what God had done for him and his master, he didn't run and tell a friend. He didn't just smile and move on. He didn't say, "Thank You, God!" under his breath. He actually "bowed his head and worshiped the LORD" (Genesis 24:26 ESV).

You have the same access to God as did this servant thousands of years ago. The question is are you using, celebrating, and thanking God for the blessing and power of prayer? If not, tap into that tool today. Then watch how and when God answers.

Lord, thank You for the privilege and power of prayer. Help me to pray from my heart of hearts—and bow in praise when You answer! Amen.

A Time for Silence

To everything there is a season, and a time
for every matter or purpose under heaven:
. . .a time to keep silence and a time to speak.
ECCLESIASTES 3:1, 7 AMPC

Your silence is a good thing when you are waiting to see and hear what God is going to do in a certain situation. It's your opportunity to stand back and watch without interrupting the work He is trying to do. Your chance to learn what God is going to accomplish near, in, or through you.

That's what Abraham's servant did. When looking for a bride for his master's son Isaac, the servant first prayed to God, saying, "Now may it be that the girl to whom I say, 'Please let down your jar so that I may drink,' and who answers, 'Drink, and I will water your camels also'—may she be the one whom You have appointed for Your servant Isaac" (Genesis 24:14 NASB). Before the servant had even finished praying to God, Rebekah showed up at the well with a water jar on her shoulder. After she filled up her water jar, the servant asked her for a drink. She gave him water to sate his thirst then drew water for his camels too. Instead of rushing ahead of God, the servant "stood gazing at her in silence, waiting to know if the Lord had made his trip prosperous" (Genesis 24:21 AMPC).

How many times have you interrupted God by speaking something into a situation when He would rather you just wait, watch, and listen until He reveals something to you?

There are times when God and those who speak for Him

want you and others to remain silent and just listen to what He has to say (Deuteronomy 27:9). There are other times when God may want you to remain in reverent silence before Him as a sign of respect for Him (Habakkuk 2:20). And there may be moments when God wants you to remain silent so that you can hear the counsel of others (Job 29:21).

Often during prayer time, if you're not careful, your thoughts can easily wander, straying into foreign territory all the while God is vying for your attention, wanting you to hear all He wants and needs to tell you. Those stray thoughts impinge upon the silence God wants you to maintain so that you can hear His voice, what He would have you do, loud and clear. Hence, Psalm 37:7 (MSG): "Quiet down before GOD, be prayerful before him."

There are also times when you are to *break* your silence. This is when you may need to confess something to God (Psalm 32:3) or speak up for yourself or others (Proverbs 31:9; Isaiah 1:17) against an injustice. It is then that God would have your voice heard.

Lord, give me wisdom to know when to speak and when to remain silent and to realize the blessings of each. Amen.

Be Still with God

Let be and be still, and know (recognize and understand) that I am God.
PSALM 46:10 AMPC

Some psalms burst with hope and power. They make the sagging spirit sing, give comfort to the troubled soul, and shore up the frightened heart. Psalm 46 is that kind of psalm.

The psalmist begins with the fact that "God is our Refuge and Strength" (verse 1 AMPC). Nothing and no one is mightier than He is. *This* God is the one you want with you in times of trouble. In fact, He is such a great and powerful God that no matter what happens, you needn't fear anything—not even when the ground shifts beneath you and the mountains fall into the sea. Not even when the seawater foams and the mountains quake at the sea's rising. Because God has you covered. He is in control.

God has a river that will give you the peace you need in times of turmoil. He moves you from whirlpools of anxiety to His gently flowing streams. God is in your midst, looking out for you, keeping you safe, calm, cool, and collected.

Nations can rage all they want. Kingdoms and governments can fall. They're not more powerful than the God who can melt the earth just by speaking. That's the kind of power the Lord of lords has. And this same all-powerful Lord *is with you*! He and His heavenly host defend and protect you. He is your refuge, in this life and the next. You, a follower of God, are invited to see all that He has done. How He creates and destroys, stops wars, destroys weapons, and burns chariots with fire.

You may know all these truths or be familiar with them. But do you then do what God wants you to do? When you go to God, can you just "let be and be still"? Can you pull yourself away from all the overwhelming sadness, trouble, and turmoil of the world and understand that you are a child of the Most High God? Can you still not just your body but the thoughts in your mind when you come before the one who holds such power over His creation?

God desires you to surrender all that you are, all that is happening in your life, and come before Him in stillness. To let the world's and your own troubles just fall away as you focus on the Lord of light and love, the one who wants a relationship with you that is tender, sweet, secure, strong, and rewarding for you both.

Each day, find time to let be and be still, to just be with God, your "High Tower and Stronghold" (Psalm 46:11 AMPC) in this life and the next.

Lord, as I come before You today, calm my heart, soothe my soul, and help me let go of my thoughts as I let be, be still, and know You are God. Amen.

It's All Good

The Lord blessed the Egyptian's house for Joseph's sake.
Genesis 39:5 ESV

Imagine you were your daddy's girl. That out of all the other children, you were the one most favored by him. Then you start having dreams, ones you've interpreted to mean that your father and siblings will one day bow to you! And then, seemingly out of nowhere, your siblings decide they're tired of you being first in Dad's affections and they've had it with your uppity attitude. So they take measured steps to remove you from their lives and the life of your father as well. The next thing you know, you're in a foreign country, working like a slave for strangers.

You might very well wonder, *Where is God in this scenario? Why doesn't He do something to help me?*

Perhaps the dire straits you now find yourself in are exactly where God wants you to be. Because if you hadn't been removed from your daddy's presence, you might forget about God and become a brat, wasting your life away when your Lord has bigger and better plans for you, your family, and the world!

Joseph fits all the criteria of the daddy's girl scenario, except that he was a daddy's boy. As a result, his jealous brothers got rid of him, selling him to some Ishmaelites who took Joseph to Egypt. There he was bought by Potiphar, one of Pharaoh's officers.

Things were going well for Joseph in his new position—so well, in fact, that Potiphar and his household were blessed "for Joseph's sake." All was well until Potiphar's indiscreet wife, tired of being slighted by Joseph, yelled "rape!" and got her revenge when Joseph was put in prison. Yet even there, "the LORD was with him. And whatever he did, the LORD made it succeed" (Genesis 39:23 ESV).

No matter what happened to Joseph or where he was sent, the Lord gave him success, blessing him and those for whom he literally slaved! Because Joseph trusted God, he didn't get depressed, angry, bitter, or anxious. Instead, his strong and steady faith—regardless of his actual circumstances—continued to keep him close to the God of blessings. Such an attitude is what brought Joseph to become Pharaoh's right-hand man, putting him in a position to help not only the Egyptians but Joseph's entire family. And it brought Joseph to tell his brothers, "You meant evil against me, but God meant it for good, to bring it about that many people should be kept alive" (Genesis 50:20 ESV).

Just as God had a plan for Joseph, He has one for you. Simply trust Him, knowing that despite all the twists and turns your life may take, God will bring it all to a good end, one that will bless you and others.

Help me, Lord, to remember that no matter what happens, You will be with me and make something good come out of it. In Jesus' name, amen.

The Secret of the Secret Place

He who dwells in the secret place of the Most High shall remain stable and fixed under the shadow of the Almighty [Whose power no foe can withstand]. I will say of the Lord, He is my Refuge and my Fortress, my God; on Him I lean and rely, and in Him I [confidently] trust!

Psalm 91:1–2 AMPC

What can you do when you are plopped down on a planet where keeping your head above water becomes more and more challenging every day? You find another residence. A hideout where you can dwell safe and secure. Only there will you find sure footing, protection, provision, and all the love you can stand. Only there will you find your true refuge and fortress in the only God you can lean on and trust.

If you abide in that secret place of the Most High, you'll find a myriad of blessings. You'll be safe from traps and diseases. You will be covered by God's huge outstretched arms (or wings) of protection. And He'll work full-time, acting as "a safe-covering and a strong wall" (Psalm 91:4 NLV).

When you dwell in God, your fears and anxieties will fall away. You won't be afraid of unseen enemies like viruses that stalk people in the darkness, nor of the problems that creep into your daytime working hours.

While others around you are falling by the thousands, you'll remain untouched—because you live in such closeness with God, protected and loved where you are. But that's not all! God "will tell His angels to care for you and keep you in all your ways. They will hold you up in their hands. So your foot will not hit against a stone" (Psalm 91:11–12 NLV).

The sweetest part of this arrangement is expressed this way by God:

> *Because he has loved Me, I will bring him out of trouble. I will set him in a safe place on high, because he has known My name. He will call upon Me, and I will answer him. I will be with him in trouble. I will take him out of trouble and honor him. I will please him with a long life. And I will show him My saving power.* (Psalm 91:14–16 NLV)

If you are looking for a way out of the worry, bad news, anxiety, and turmoil of this life on earth, get a new perspective on life by looking up. God is waiting for you to join Him in that secret place. To dwell there with Him, allowing the all-powerful one to be what He longs to be: your refuge and fortress. Your loving God.

Thank You, Lord, for offering me such a wonderful place to live and breathe. Lift me up now, Most High God. For You alone are my refuge and fortress. In Jesus' name I pray, amen.

Honoring God Above All

God was pleased with the midwives. The people continued to increase in number—a very strong people. And because the midwives honored God, God gave them families of their own.

Exodus 1:20–21 MSG

Just as God had promised, His people multiplied to the point that Egypt was filled with them. The only problem was that the new pharaoh in town had no idea who Joseph was or what he had done for his adopted country. So Pharaoh decided that, for national security purposes, the strength and number of God's people needed to be curtailed. To accomplish that, the Israelites were made slaves and used to build cities. Yet the more Pharaoh and his people abused and misused God's people, the greater their number grew!

Pharaoh then came up with another idea. He went to the Hebrew midwives—Shiphrah and Puah—telling them, "When you serve as midwife to the Hebrew women and see them on the birthstool, if it is a son, you shall kill him, but if it is a daughter, she shall live" (Exodus 1:16 ESV). There was only one problem with this new form of Jewish "birth control": The midwives were more afraid of God than they were of Pharaoh. So, firm in their courage and commitment to God and their people, the midwives ignored Pharaoh's command.

When Pharaoh asked the midwives why they let the male newborns live, they told him, "Because the Hebrew women are not like the Egyptian women, for they are vigorous and give birth before the midwife comes to them" (Exodus 1:19 ESV). Because of the midwives' actions (or rather their inactions) and because they did the right thing in God's eyes, God blessed them with families of their own.

Yet Pharaoh was not to be duped. Thus, his only recourse was to enlist the help of his people to curb the Israelite population. This is the scenario painted of Egypt in the days just before Moses was to enter this realm as a newborn babe.

God loves to make the enemies of His people look like fools. And that's just what He did in this story. For not only do His people continue to grow in number, but they end up getting one over on Pharaoh by creating a situation in which one of their own male Hebrew babies (i.e., Moses) becomes not only the adopted grandchild of Pharaoh himself but the one who would lead the Israelites, along with much of their adopted country's riches, out of Egypt! Yet none of this would have been possible if the Hebrew midwives had feared Pharaoh more than their own God.

Where and when have your courage and commitment led you to do the right thing in God's eyes?

Lord, give me the courage to walk with You,
no matter where You take me or the challenges
I may face once I get there. Amen.

Carried Away by God

You have seen how the Lord your God bore you, as a man carries his son, in all the way that you went until you came to this place.
DEUTERONOMY 1:31 AMPC

When a toddler is hurt, afraid, or just needs some tender loving care, chances are the first person he'll run to is his mother. For she's the one who carried him from the beginning, before he fully entered the world. The first words out of the toddler's mouth might be "Up, up," for he knows where his place of safety lies: in his mother's arms.

As the years go by, the child begins to garner his own strength and power. The bigger the boy grows, the further away he gets. Soon he's relying on his own strength and power. And that's when the fallacy of self-sufficiency comes into play.

When we become adults, we start to believe we don't need our mother's hands to soothe us. That's usually a good thing. But problems may begin when we start to believe we can handle anything that comes our way. That we can carry ourselves and our own burdens, pull ourselves up out of any pit of trouble, make our own way in the world. That we no longer need anyone's help. Right? Wrong.

Much of the stress, angst, and anxiety we suffer is preventable. All we need to do is give up the idea that we don't need anyone to help us, to recognize there is an all-powerful being who longs to pick us up, love us, shelter us, protect us, and, best of all, carry us. That's why God and Jesus continually tell us they are willing and wanting to hold us tightly in their arms.

Through Isaiah, God tells you, "Behold, the Lord God will come with might, and His arm will rule for Him. Behold, His reward is with Him, and His recompense before Him. He will feed His flock like a shepherd: He will gather the lambs in His arm, He will carry them in His bosom" (Isaiah 40:10–11 AMPC). With one strong arm, God rules over all. With the other, He gathers you up, holds you close to His heart, and carries you.

During an epidemic, you may have to distance yourself from the most vulnerable people, some of whom may be children. For the first time, you may realize your arms are no longer the safest place for those you love. Yet don't despair. For you know the best, safest, and most healing and hopeful place to be is in God's arms—today and every day.

I'm weary and afraid, Lord. I need a safe place to rest, a loving arm to hold me, someone to carry me for a bit. So I'm coming to You, Lord, saying, "Up, up!" Lift me into Your arms. Hold me tight. Surround me with Your love. In Jesus' name, amen.

A Mother's Courage and a Sister's Cunning

When she could hide him no longer, she took for him a basket made of bulrushes and daubed it with bitumen and pitch. She put the child in it and placed it among the reeds by the river bank. And his sister stood at a distance to know what would be done to him.

EXODUS 2:3–4 ESV

Jochebed and her husband, Amram, were both from the priestly house of Levi. Jochebed had already birthed two children, Aaron and Miriam. Now she was pregnant once more, this time with Moses. This was in the days when Pharaoh and his kill-all-newborn-Hebrew-boys order was on the books.

When Moses was born, Jochebed worked to hide him for three months. But she knew she couldn't do so forever. So she made a watertight basket for him, placed Moses in it, and put it among the reeds in the Nile River.

Miriam stood some distance away, waiting to see what would happen to her baby brother. As Miriam watched, Pharaoh's daughter with her entourage came down to the river to bathe. It was she who spied the basket containing Moses and sent a servant to fetch it. When she opened it and saw Moses inside, she knew he was one of the Hebrew children, yet he was so beautiful that he immediately captured her heart.

After approaching the princess, Miriam asked if she should call one of the Hebrew women to nurse the child for the princess.

Seeing the wisdom of this proposal, "Pharaoh's daughter said to her, Go. And the girl went and called the child's mother" (Exodus 2:8 AMPC). Pharaoh's daughter told Jochebed to nurse Moses and to bring him back when he was weaned. That's how Moses became Pharaoh's adopted grandson and was brought up in a king's house. But it's certain Jochebed continued to have an influence over the boy, for he never forgot his Hebrew heritage.

Moses was born in a treacherous era for Hebrew male newborns. Yet Jochebed managed not only to give him life but to hide him long enough to find a safe way of keeping him alive. Miriam used her cunning to arrange for her mother to nurse her own child—and be paid for doing it! Both women had waited until the right moment to protect Moses and give him the best life they could. Because of their faith and God's wisdom, Moses was blessed.

Your blessings don't depend on your circumstances. They depend on knowing and believing your God is always good. And with that thought in your mind and heart, even when you may not feel blessed, the truth of the matter is that you are.

Good God of all, help me remember that with You in my heart, I am and always will be blessed. For You are in my life, working Your will for the good of all—including me! Amen.

God's Provision

God called to him from inside the bush, saying, "Moses, Moses!" Moses answered, "Here I am."

EXODUS 3:4 NLV

After murdering an Egyptian for beating up a Hebrew slave, Moses ran away to Midian. There he started a family and became a shepherd over the flock of his father-in-law, Jethro.

While Moses was away, the old pharaoh died. And the cries of God's people reached God's ears.

One day while Moses was watching Jethro's sheep, he came to Horeb. And there God appeared to him in the form of a burning bush.

God tells Moses he needs to rescue the people of Israel and take them to the Promised Land. But Moses begins making all the excuses he can think of as to why he's not the man for the job. After all, who in their right mind would want to travel back to a country where they're wanted for murder?

Thus, when God tells Moses everything he needs to do to save His people, Moses asks, "Who am I to go to Pharaoh and bring the people of Israel out of Egypt?" (Exodus 3:11 NLV). God answers, "But I will be with you" (Exodus 3:12 NLV).

Moses then asks, "What if they ask who sent me? What am I to tell them so that they don't think I'm nuts?" God says, *"Just tell them I AM WHO I AM sent you."*

Moses then asks, "What if they will not believe me or listen to me? They might say, 'The Lord has not shown Himself to you'" (Exodus 4:1 NLV). God asks Moses to throw his staff on the ground. When he does, the stick turns into a snake. God tells him to pick it up by the tail. Moses does, and the snake becomes a stick once more. God then tells Moses to put his hand in his coat. Moses does, and his hand becomes white. God then tells him to put it in his coat again. Moses does, and his hand returns to normal. Then God tells Moses that if they still don't believe him, all he has to do is pour some Nile water on the ground and the water will turn into blood.

Moses then tells God he's not a good speaker. God tells him He will be with Moses and tell him what to say.

Finally, Moses puts it all on the line, asking God to send someone else. That is the proverbial last straw as God's anger burns against Moses. Through perhaps gritted teeth, God tells Moses his brother, Aaron, can speak for him. He's on his way to see Moses already.

When God calls you, He also equips you, blessing you with exactly what you need to do work in His will.

When You call me into action, Lord, remind me You will also give me what I need to do Your will Your way. So all I need to say in reply is "Yes, Lord, yes." Amen.

God's Got This

Fear not; stand still (firm, confident, undismayed) and see the salvation of the Lord which He will work for you today. For the Egyptians you have seen today you shall never see again. The Lord will fight for you, and you shall hold your peace and remain at rest.

EXODUS 14:13–14 AMPC

Have you ever found yourself wedged between a rock and a hard place? That can be a very uncomfortable situation. But with God, there's always a perfect solution, a fitting way out of any predicament.

Consider Moses. He'd gone back to Egypt. And after several miracles worked through him and his brother, Aaron, Moses had not convinced Pharaoh to free God's people. Until that last plague, the Passover when the firstborn son of all but the Israelites died. Then the Egyptians not only begged the Israelites to leave but gave them whatever they asked!

After Moses had gotten God's people out, "God did not lead them by way of the land of the Philistines, although that was near" (Exodus 13:17 ESV). God was concerned that if the people encountered a battle, they would want to hightail it back to Egypt. So God took the Israelites the long way around via the wilderness and toward the Red Sea, leading them in a pillar of cloud by day and a pillar of fire at night.

As the Israelites make camp by the sea, Pharaoh decides to rescind his order to allow them to go free. Gathering his soldiers, chariots, and horses, Pharaoh and his army chase down the Israelites, trapping them between the approaching army and the water.

That's where Moses gives God's people some very powerful words. He says, *"Listen, people. Do not be afraid. Simply stand still. Have firm confidence in God. And just watch and see how He works for you today. These people, these Egyptians you see today? You'll never see them again. God is going to fight this battle for you All you need to do is be quiet. Relax. He's got this. He's got you."*

God is speaking to you today, giving you this same message. No matter what comes against you, don't worry. Don't be afraid. Just stand still wherever you are. The God who created you has got you covered. This problem you're worried about? It's on its way out the door. You'll never see it again.

Speak Your good word into my life today, Lord. Help me keep worry at bay by remembering that because You are with me, I need not be afraid. These troubles that are here today will not darken my door again. So I stand here, Lord, still. Quiet. Because You've got this. Amen.

Oh, the Thoughts You Can Think

Finally, brothers, whatever is true, whatever is honorable, whatever is just, whatever is pure, whatever is lovely, whatever is commendable, if there is any excellence, if there is anything worthy of praise, think about these things.

PHILIPPIANS 4:8 ESV

One of the most profound truths in God's Word is found in Proverbs 23:7 (NLV): "For as he thinks in his heart, so is he." The apostle Paul may have had this proverb in mind when he wrote the letter to the church in Philippi while in prison in Rome. He must have known from experience that you need to be aware of what thoughts are running through your head. For if you don't, chances are anxiety and depression will overtake not just your mind but your life.

You're not to let your thoughts lead you astray. Paul urged his Roman readers, "Do not be conformed to this world, but be transformed by the renewal of your mind, that by testing you may discern what is the will of God, what is good and acceptable and perfect" (Romans 12:2 ESV).

So what should you think about—what thoughts should occupy a mind that does not want to be claimed by the flesh but by the Spirit? Philippians 4:8 (MSG) gives you a pretty good list: "You'll do best by filling your minds and meditating on things true, noble, reputable, authentic, compelling, gracious—the best, not the worst; the beautiful, not the ugly; things to praise, not things to curse." When you focus your mind on the truth, your thoughts won't be swept away by rumors, gossip, or just plain lies. (And you know who the "father of lies" is, right? John 8:44 tells us he's the devil.) And none of those things does your body—or your life—good.

You're to think about things that are right, pure, admirable, and praiseworthy. That sounds much better than thinking about things that are untrue, impure, shameful, and disreputable, doesn't it?

Think of things that are worth thinking about. Things that will improve your mind and life. Things that will lift up you so that you, in turn, can lift up others.

Today, make an effort to be conscious of your thoughts, where your mind might be going, straying. Then use this list from Philippians 4:8 as a litmus test so you can see where your mind might be leading you down a dark path. For when you examine your thoughts and renew them when needed, you'll be blessed with God's peace.

Help me, Lord, to keep a sharp lookout on my thoughts. Bring to my mind Your own worthy words, ones I can use to lift up myself and others. Help me keep my mind on You, Lord. For then I know I will have peace of mind. Amen.

The Eagle That Soars

Those who wait for the Lord [who expect, look for, and hope in Him] shall change and renew their strength and power; they shall lift their wings and mount up [close to God] as eagles [mount up to the sun]; they shall run and not be weary, they shall walk and not faint or become tired.

ISAIAH 40:31 AMPC

Life can be more than difficult at times. There are heartaches, unexpected losses, faded dreams, and disappointments. Yet even through all the upheavals and downturns life hands us, we can still have hope, courage, strength, and peace of mind, heart, spirit, and soul. These blessings come by waiting on God, expecting Him to intervene in the matters you face. For in God alone can you find the unfathomable and unlimited strength, power, satisfaction, and peace you crave.

Speaking through Isaiah, God describes those who wait on Him to take action as eagles that renew their strength and power in Him, that lift their wings and rise up, flying close to Him. God says people who hope and wait for Him will run and not get weary, walk and not get tired.

So how does a woman get from worried to weariless? By looking up instead of down. By allowing her thoughts to lift her spirit instead of crushing it.

Yet what about all the things that are wrong in this world? The injustices, the abuses of power, the racial and gender inequalities? Put them in God's hands. Trust Him to take care of that which is out of your hands—or trust Him to show you what you can do as His hands and feet on this earth.

The life of Gladys Aylward, a Christian missionary to China, is covered in the book *The Small Woman* by Alan Burgess and has been made into the film *The Inn of the Sixth Happiness*. Against all odds—all logic, obstacles, and expectations—Gladys managed to go from a maid in London to a revered and well-loved missionary in Yangcheng, China. There, along with an older missionary, Jeannie Lawson, she established the Inn of the Eight Happinesses where they not only provided bed and board for travelers but shared stories about Jesus.

Eventually, Gladys adopted several orphans. When the region was infiltrated by the Japanese army, she led more than one hundred orphans to safety over treacherous terrain. Gladys once said, "The eagle that soars in the upper air does not worry itself as to how to cross rivers."

No matter the size of your worries and concerns, be as the eagle. Fly above them, knowing that as you wait on God, He will give you the strength and power you need to fly closer to Him and further from your troubles.

Lord, help me be as the eagle. Help me develop wings of trust, hope, and patience as I fly ever closer to You. In Jesus' name, amen.

On Becoming

I would have despaired unless I had believed that I would see the goodness of the LORD in the land of the living. Wait for the LORD; be strong and let your heart take courage.

PSALM 27:13–14 NASB

What would you like to become in this life? A worrywart continually biting her lip or a gentlewoman exuding peace of mind and heart? The latter, no doubt. Yet many of us are not born calm, cool, and collected. But no need to worry. For you can look to God to give you the belief, hope, and expectation that even amid darkness, trouble, and evil, you will see His goodness in your current world.

Have no doubt that God can make proverbial lemonade out of lemons. Believe that God will do something good. Then *look* for it. Look for the light within the dark, the gold within the sediment, the silver lining in the cloud.

Looking for the good does not mean you're ignoring the bad or are blind to the miseries of others. It may mean you pray. Prayer, along with praise, is the most anyone can do for herself, others, and her environment. For your prayers are not temporary but eternal! As Abraham Lincoln said, "I remember my mother's prayers and they have always followed me. They have clung to me all my life." That mother, that woman, is one powerful prayer. As are you. You too can pray prayers that will cling to people the rest of their lives.

Today, begin looking for that silver lining in every cloud you encounter. Be determined to find the light amid the darkness, the gold within the gunk. Aim to become that woman of prayer, the one who looks for the best in everything and everyone. Using the power of scripture, change your mind from pessimist to optimist. In fact, look for another way to express Psalm 27:13–14. Perhaps use the verses in the English Standard Version of the Bible: "I believe that I shall look upon the goodness of the LORD in the land of the living! Wait for the LORD; be strong, and let your heart take courage; wait for the LORD!" Or go with The Message for an even more optimistic take on today's verse: "I'm sure now I'll see God's goodness in the exuberant earth. Stay with GOD! Take heart. Don't quit. I'll say it again: Stay with GOD." At the beginning, middle, and end of every day, repeat these verses in whatever translation your heart may be drawn to. And as you go throughout your day, actively look for God's goodness, expecting to see it come your way. And it will!

Lord, I believe I will see Your goodness today, here, in the land of the living. Open my eyes to see Your blessings. And help me compose prayers to pray wherever the darkness in this world needs Your light. In Jesus' name I pray and praise, amen.

While Still Praying

While I was speaking and praying. . .while I was still speaking in prayer, then the man Gabriel, whom I had seen in the vision previously, came to me in my extreme weariness about the time of the evening offering.

DANIEL 9:20–21 NASB

How would your prayer life change if you made it a certainty in your mind and heart that before you even *begin* to pray, God answers; that while you're still speaking, God hears your words? God makes that amazing promise to believers in Isaiah 65:24! And even better, that same promise proved true for Daniel, the Israelite determined to follow God even though he had been deported to Babylon.

Daniel had been reading from the book of Jeremiah. There he learned the Jews' captivity in Babylon would last seventy years! So Daniel went to God humbly, while fasting, wearing sackcloth and ashes. He gave his "attention to the Lord God to seek Him by prayer and supplications" (Daniel 9:3 NASB).

Through his prayers, Daniel admitted right away that his country had sinned against God. At times, even rebelled. That they hadn't listened to God's prophets. He also made it clear he was praying not according to what he and his people were nor what they had done, but according to who God Himself had proven to be and who He still is—a compassionate God who longs to lead His people in righteousness.

While Daniel was still praying, before he had stopped speaking, asking for forgiveness, asking for God to open His ears to his pleas, the angel Gabriel arrived! He came to Daniel right around the time of the evening sacrifice and told him, "I have now come to give you wisdom and understanding. As soon as you began to pray, an answer was given, which I have come to tell you. For you are loved very much. So listen to what I say and understand the special dream" (Daniel 9:22–23 NLV).

Imagine taking your deepest, most heartfelt requests to God, laying them and yourself at His feet, admitting your mistakes and foibles, and telling Him exactly what you need. *And while you're still praying, still speaking to God*, you hear a fluttering of wings and realize God is at that very moment ready to not just speak to your heart but give an answer to your plea.

Imagine living a life knowing God's answer is less than a prayer away from your lips.

God always comes through on His promises. And this promise is sure to change not just your prayer habits but your very life.

Lord, You are amazing. Nothing is beyond Your will, power, or pleasure as You lead me ever closer to Your plan for me. Help me, Lord, to pray with the knowledge that before I even start to pray, Your answer is already winging its way to me. In Jesus' name, amen.

According to Plan

"For I know the plans I have for you, declares the Lord, plans for welfare and not for evil, to give you a future and a hope."

JEREMIAH 29:11 ESV

Do you know God has a plan for your life? Do you *really* know it? Do you think about that when you wake up each morning? Do you find it easy to rest with that truth, the promise that God has a certain future and hope for you? Do you believe that whatever His plans may be, they are for your good and not your bad?

It may be that deep down you know God has a plan for you, but you don't necessarily consider that truth when you wake up each day. After all, you have a lot on your mind. So much is going on in the world, both things that seem to be under your control, up to a certain point, and things way beyond your control. And all you're really trying to do is make your way through that maze of thoughts within based on what you experience without—on both good days and bad.

Perhaps when you pray each morning, you're forgetting to tailor your plans or consider them to be subject to whatever *God's* overall plan may be for you. After all, He *is* God. He's the one who has the wisdom. He's the one who knows the beginning, middle, and end of your story. He's the one who knows the particular part you're to play in His grand plan.

It might be you don't really trust God as much as He'd like you to. Maybe there's something of your own will that you're holding back from Him because you have some doubts about this whole arrangement with the Creator of the world.

If any of these scenarios ring true for you, it's time to change things up. Begin by growing your faith and trust in God. Reach back into your mind or your journal to see how often God has come through for you. Memorize some Bible verses, ones like Isaiah 26:3 (ESV): "You keep him in perfect peace whose mind is stayed on you, because he trusts in you." Try to personalize such verses, making them closer to what you can say in your heart and pray back to God: "You, Lord, give me perfect peace when I keep my thoughts, my mind and heart, on You, because I *do* trust in You. Help me grow that trust and see it increase day by day."

Also consider making your plans dependent upon God's bigger plans.

Lord, as I consider my plans for today, remind me every moment that You have a bigger plan that holds greater sway over my life. To Your plans I bow, understanding and thanking You that Your plans are always for my best and You will give me the wisdom to discern what You would have me do in every instance. Amen.

Less Stuff, More God

Don't be obsessed with getting more material things. Be relaxed with what you have. Since God assured us, "I'll never let you down, never walk off and leave you," we can boldly quote, God is there, ready to help; I'm fearless no matter what. Who or what can get to me?

HEBREWS 13:5–6 MSG

God doesn't want you obsessed with getting more "stuff." Why? Because God wants you focused and dependent on Him—and Him alone! He wants you to use any "excess" of things or money you might have to support your church and/or those who don't have enough to make ends meet. But to be able to rely on God and no one or nothing else, you must trust Him to always be there. And that, at times, can be the most difficult part.

This idea of believing that God will never let you down, that He will never, *ever* leave you, may be challenging for some people, especially those who have been disappointed by other human beings before. Perhaps a parent died when the person was young. Or Mom and Dad divorced. Perhaps her own spouse abandoned her. Or the friends she counted on deserted her during a time of trouble. The problem here is that a comparison is being made between fallible people and the perfectly infallible Creator. And that is *no* comparison. For God is not a human being who makes a mistake here and there. God is the one who created this world, this universe, and you. He has a grand plan for everyone on this planet—including you, His very own child. So who are you to refute Him?

To build up your trust and confidence in the God who will never let you down or leave you, consider memorizing some Bible verses that support that truth. Here are a few to start you off:

> "For I the Lord your God hold your right hand; I am the Lord, Who says to you, Fear not; I will help you!" (Isaiah 41:13 AMPC).
>
> "Even when you are old I will be the same. And even when your hair turns white, I will help you. I will take care of what I have made. I will carry you, and will save you" (Isaiah 46:4 NLV).
>
> "He won't let you stumble, your Guardian God won't fall asleep. Not on your life! Israel's Guardian will never doze or sleep" (Psalm 121:3–4 MSG).

Today and every day, rely on the one who will always be with you, watching over you, loving you. And you'll find yourself more relaxed, at peace, and full of joy than you ever knew possible. For trusting in Him is His will for you.

Thank You, Lord, for all You do for me. May I trust in and rely on You every moment of this life—in heaven and on earth. In Jesus' name, amen.

Your Words Were Heard

Then he said to me, Fear not, Daniel, for from the first day that you set your mind and heart to understand and to humble yourself before your God, your words were heard, and I have come as a consequence of [and in response to] your words.

DANIEL 10:12 AMPC

Words—spoken, written, or thought—wield great power. They can make or break humans. That's why we must be careful with the words we use, for the words that fall on another's ears or enter into another's mind can either bless or curse another being.

Daniel was an exile from Judah who was now serving a king in Babylon. From the very beginning of his captivity, he had determined to continue following God. "Daniel resolved that he would not defile himself with the king's food, or with the wine that he drank" (Daniel 1:8 ESV). Once Daniel determined to follow God—no matter where he was or what his condition or prospects—"God gave Daniel favor and compassion in the sight of the chief of the eunuchs" (Daniel 1:9 ESV). Yet the blessings didn't stop there, for God gave Daniel and his three friends all the wisdom, understanding, and knowledge they needed for all things, including interpreting dreams and visions (Daniel 1:17).

Because Daniel determined to abide by God's law and humbly worship Him outside Judah, because he resolved to do all he could to continue down the road with his Lord, because he chose to set his mind and heart to understand God, the Lord of all heard his prayers and responded by sending him help.

How have you determined to live your life? Have you set your mind and heart not just to be humble before God but to work to understand Him as well? Of course, some aspects of God's character will always be way beyond what human minds can process or comprehend. Still, there is so much value in understanding God, in knowing who He is.

For the more you understand and know God, the more you can grow spiritually. The closer you get to Him, the clearer your pathway will become.

Besides all that, God *demands* you know Him better, saying, "Be still, and know that I am God" (Psalm 46:10 ESV). And that's something you can brag about! Why? Because God says so: "If you brag, brag of this and this only: That you understand and know me. I'm God, and I act in loyal love. I do what's right and set things right and fair, and delight in those who do the same things. These are my trademarks" (Jeremiah 9:24 MSG).

I am determined, Lord, to know You better and better every day. Please reveal Yourself to me in this moment. Show me what You would have me know. In Jesus' name, amen.

Day by Day

Blessed be the Lord, Who bears our burdens and carries us day by day, even the God Who is our salvation! Selah [pause, and calmly think of that]!
PSALM 68:19 AMPC

The sun rises and so do you, ready to face a new day, make a fresh mark on the minutes to come. But then those thoughts enter your mind. Thoughts of yesterdays and yesteryears. Slights and snubs you experienced, doubts and discontents that linger, regrets and remarks you can't seem to bury. Before you know it, before your feet even hit the floor, you feel weighed down by the things you can't change and the things you can't forget.

Once you do pull yourself up from the mattress, your back is bent over, aching with the weight of choices made yesterday and the burden of disappointments rooted in would'ves, should'ves, and could'ves; fears of tomorrow; and vain imaginings you can't seem to shake. Making your way into the bathroom, you catch a glimpse of yourself in the mirror, and the story of the woman in Luke 13, the one who "was bent completely forward and utterly unable to straighten herself up or to look upward" (verse 11 AMPC), enters your mind. The only differences between you and her are that thousands of years have passed since she walked this earth; that you're looking in the bathroom mirror, not hanging out at the local synagogue; and that the burden on your back is one *you've* decided to hang on to instead of giving it to Jesus.

Just as Jesus saw that woman, He is seeing you, calling to

you, saying, "Woman, you are released from your infirmity!" (Luke 13:12 AMPC). And like that woman, if you put yourself in Jesus' hands, you too can instantly be made straight! Then you too will recognize, thank, and praise God.

Remember whose child you are. Remember that God bears your burdens, carrying the brunt of the weight Himself, day after day. Remember that along with bearing your burdens, God also carries you—day after day after day!

By keeping these thoughts in mind, by writing these truths on the tablet of your heart, you can tap into the calm that only God can give you. You can access His peace, the kind that surpasses all of your understanding, and allow it to "guard your heart and your mind in Christ Jesus" (see Philippians 4:7 ESV).

Today is your day to make a fresh start. In this moment, let all your doubts, misgivings, regrets, and any other weight you've been clinging to, slide off your back and land at Jesus' feet, for Him to dispose of as He wishes. Then you will realize the true peace and freedom gained in Christ.

Lord, take this weight, these burdens, off my mind, heart, and back so I may easily rise up and praise You. In Jesus' name, amen.

The Lord Is with You

"The Lord is with you, O mighty man of valor."
Judges 6:12 ESV

For seven years God allowed the Midianites to hassle the Israelites. Why? Because God's people kept making the wrong choices, doing what they thought was right in their own eyes rather than doing what was right in *God's* eyes.

Things got so bad the Israelites made dens in the mountains and caves so they would be better hidden and protected from the Midianites. God's people also had trouble feeding themselves because as soon as they'd plant a crop, their enemy would come in and destroy it. So, once again, the Israelites cried out to God. And once again He answered. But the person God chose to lead His people didn't seem to be a likely candidate—especially to the candidate himself!

The leader God selected was beating out his wheat in a winepress, hiding his produce, his task, and himself from the Midianite raiders. The angel of the Lord took a seat under a tree that belonged to Gideon's dad and said to him, "The Lord is with you, O mighty man of valor."

In our eyes, Gideon doesn't seem like a man of courage. After all, he's *hiding* from the Midianites. And here God is calling him a "mighty man of valor." How off base can God be? But, as He shows us time and time again, God knows who He created us to be. It's we ourselves who sometimes need to have our value called out.

Gideon responds to God with a question we've all probably

asked Him at some point in time: "Please, my lord, if the LORD is with us, why then has all this happened to us? And where are all his wonderful deeds that our fathers recounted?" (Judges 6:13 ESV). But God doesn't answer Gideon's question. Instead He tells him, "Go in this might of yours and save Israel from the hand of Midian; do not I send you?" (Judges 6:14 ESV).

This is when Gideon asks God, "How can I, of all people, save my country?" The problem here is that when Gideon looks at himself, he doesn't see what God sees. Where God sees a "mighty man of valor," Gideon sees his clan as being the weakest and he himself as being the least in his father's house. And here is where we and Gideon are given the gift of God's response, a wondrous truth that makes all the difference in his life and ours: "But I will be with you" (Judges 6:16 ESV).

God already sees you as the woman He created you to be. To become that woman, all you need to remember is that God is with you. And with Him by your side, you can do and become all He calls you to do and become.

Lord, thank You for being with me. Work in my life to help me become who You've created me to be. In Jesus' name, amen.

Your Desired Haven

They cry to the Lord in their trouble, and He brings them out of their distresses. He hushes the storm to a calm and to a gentle whisper, so that the waves of the sea are still. Then the men are glad because of the calm, and He brings them to their desired haven.

PSALM 107:28–30 AMPC

It had been a long day. Jesus had healed so many people. Then, with the help of a small boy who had five loaves of bread and two small fish, Jesus fed a crowd of over five thousand men, plus the women and children with them. But as the crowd started getting the idea of making Him king, Jesus went off by Himself to pray on a hillside.

Jesus' disciples, meanwhile, headed down to the Sea of Galilee. They'd decided to cross the sea in a boat, even though Jesus still hadn't rejoined them. Off they sailed, heading into the darkness. Soon the sea began getting rough because of a violent wind.

As they strained at the oars, having rowed about three to four miles, the disciples saw Jesus. He was walking on the water, heading toward their boat! They were terrified! So Jesus told them, "It is I; do not be afraid" (John 6:20 ESV).

Realizing the apparition was Jesus, the disciples were more than happy to have Him climb into their boat. "Now the boat went at once to the land they had steered toward. [And immediately they reached the shore toward which they had been slowly making their way]" (John 6:21 AMPC).

The account of this boating incident in John 6 bears a striking resemblance to its precursor in Psalm 107:23–30. There, the text is about sailors on the sea who get into trouble, so much trouble that "their courage melts away because of their plight" (Psalm 107:26 AMPC). But there too, God sees His people's plight, hears their cries for help, and responds to their dilemma. He hushes the storm, and the waves still. Then, just like Jesus, Father God brings them to their desired haven, the destination they had been struggling to reach.

Woman of the Way, whenever you are straining to reach a destination or frightened by the storm you find yourself in, cry out to God, ask Him for help, invite Him into your boat, and hand the tiller to Him. Before you know it, He'll be there, calming the storm, stilling the waves, and bringing you toward that desired haven, the one toward which you've been slowly making your way.

You, Lord, are so wonderful. Thank You for hearing my cries, responding so quickly, and helping me get to where we'd both have me be. In Jesus' name, amen.

Never Spent

"Thus says the LORD, the God of Israel, 'The jar of flour shall not be spent, and the jug of oil shall not be empty, until the day that the LORD sends rain upon the earth.' "

1 KINGS 17:14 ESV

Just when you think you're stuck, God enters through a window you hadn't noticed before. The next thing you know, your life has changed—for your good and His glory.

That's what happened to a widow who was picking up sticks when Elijah came along. But let's go back a bit further. . .

Elijah the prophet had just told the evil king Ahab that, according to God, there wouldn't be any rain for a while. Then God told Elijah to go to the brook Cherith. For God—who has power over all creation—was going to send some ravens to feed him there. Twice a day ravens brought Elijah bread and meat for food, and he drank from the brook. When the brook dried up, God told Elijah to head to Zarephath, where He'd arranged for a widow to provide for him.

So Elijah went. At the gate to the city, he saw a woman picking up some sticks. He asked her for some water. As she went to fulfill his request, Elijah added to his order: "While you're up, bring me back some bread too. Okay?"

That's when the widow told him she didn't have any bread. All she had was some flour in a jar and some oil in a jug. Her plan had been to use those meager provisions to make a final meal for herself and her son. Then they could die.

That was the woman's *perceived* ending to her and her son's story. But it wasn't the one God had in mind. Elijah told the woman the three-word command God wants all His followers to obey: "Do not fear." Then Elijah told her to make some bread for him first and then make something for her and her son. Because God said, "The jar of flour shall not be spent, and the jug of oil shall not be empty, until the day that the LORD sends rain upon the earth" (1 Kings 17:14 ESV). The widow obeyed Elijah's directions, and she and her son ate for many days because God came through on His promise of provision.

Whenever you feel as if your story, dreams, goals, or plans are coming to any kind of end, don't fear. Don't give up or in. Instead, pray to God. Ask Him to speak a good word into your situation. In so doing, you'll be making way for a miracle to enter your life from the God who not only will increase what little you have but also will make a way for you to share your good with others.

Thank You, Lord, for always making a way when there seems to be no way. Amen.

Facing the Fire

Blessed be the God of Shadrach, Meshach, and Abednego, Who has sent His angel and delivered His servants who believed in, trusted in, and relied on Him! And they set aside the king's command and yielded their bodies rather than serve or worship any god except their own God.

DANIEL 3:28 AMPC

Along with Daniel, three friends—Shadrach, Meshach, and Abednego—had been taken captive in Judah and brought to serve in Babylon. They'd seen the massive idol of gold—ninety feet tall and nine feet thick—that King Nebuchadnezzar had commissioned and set up on the plain of Dura in Babylon.

During the golden idol's dedication service, a herald announced, "When you hear the sound of the horn, pipe, lyre, trigon, harp, bagpipe, and every kind of music, you are to fall down and worship the golden image that King Nebuchadnezzar has set up. And whoever does not fall down and worship shall immediately be cast into a burning fiery furnace" (Daniel 3:5–6 ESV). After that, when all the people heard the music, they fell down and worshipped Nebuchadnezzar's idol. Well, all the people except for some Jews named Shadrach, Meshach, and Abednego. They refused to bow down to anything or anyone other than their Lord.

The fact that the three friends had blatantly disobeyed the king's command was brought to Nebuchadnezzar's attention, sending the king into a rage. His questioning of the men validated the report against them. Yet they refused to change their minds, even though they knew things would heat up for them in the fiery furnace. They told the king, "Our God whom we serve is able to deliver us from the burning fiery furnace, and he will deliver us. . . . But if not, be it known to you, O king, that we will not serve your gods or worship the golden image" (Daniel 3:17–18 ESV). And into the furnace they went!

Yet when the king looked into the flames, he noticed not only the three men walking around in the furnace but a fourth with them—and he looked like the Son of God! When Nebuchadnezzar ordered Shadrach, Meshach, and Abednego back out, they were not only not burned but didn't even smell of smoke!

Afterward, the king made a decree saying that anyone who spoke against the God of the three friends would be cut in pieces and their home destroyed. Then the king promoted Shadrach, Meshach, and Abednego!

When you courageously make it known that you trust in the one and only God, don't fear the consequences. For not only will you be able to face the fires you're bound to attract, but God will walk with you through the flames.

Lord, give me the courage to make my trust in You known to all, no matter the consequences. Amen.

Calm and Quiet

O LORD, my heart is not proud, nor my eyes haughty; nor do I involve myself in great matters, or in things too difficult for me. Surely I have composed and quieted my soul; like a weaned child rests against his mother, my soul is like a weaned child within me.

PSALM 131:1–2 NASB

When a mother is trying to wean her child from her breast, she's bound to face some challenges, the most difficult of which is denying her child her milk. The mother has to keep her own resolve and not give in to the cries and frustrations of her child. There may be some sleepless nights for the entire family until the babe learns how to do without that which he once petulantly demanded and soon afterward obtained.

In the weaning process, the child will find a way to quiet himself. After the initial struggle, the baby is soon just as happy simply lying against his mother's breast as he once was when he drew nourishment and satisfaction from that same breast. New doors begin opening for that child as he is now ready, willing, and able to sit at the big table with the other kids and his parents.

When following God, you too might find yourself out of sorts, fretting or becoming petulant as you begin to discover that He wants you humble and composed, that you now need to depend on God alone for your nourishment and bodily desires. You are now expected to place your hope in God's taking care of you, meeting your needs, becoming your only provider in all of life's many facets. Instead of going after what the world has to offer or getting caught up in the storms and passions of life, you have come through your own weaning period and are now ready to be content in God alone.

So how do you find this contentment, this quiet calm of a weaned child? You admit that you need God's help. You search His Word so that you can grow in trust. Each day, you find a way to let go of the difficulties that life can present and tap into the peace of God that is beyond all understanding. You let go of the fretting and fearing and take in God's peace and heavenly rest.

Begin cultivating a quiet heart today. Dive into God's Word and find the verses that will keep you composed as you live in Christ. Ask Him to gift you with the peace that He has left for His people. And soon you too will find the calm you require to quiet your own soul as you rest your head against the chest of your tender teacher.

Lord, guide me through Your Word. Help me find the passages You would have me read, ones that will help me calm and quiet my soul. In Jesus' name, amen.

The Light Within the Darkness

"Blessed be the name of God forever and ever, to whom belong wisdom and might. He changes times and seasons; he removes kings and sets up kings; he gives wisdom to the wise and knowledge to those who have understanding; he reveals deep and hidden things; he knows what is in the darkness, and the light dwells with him."

DANIEL 2:20–22 ESV

We don't know what the future holds. God tells us to trust Him for that, as well as the past and present. Yet there may be times when darkness sets in. When we cannot see our hand in front of our face. When we're afraid that any move—forward or backward—will be in the wrong direction. Yet we know we can't stay rooted to the spot where we stand.

Instead of feeling discouraged or frustrated because we don't know what the future holds, we should rest easy—our not knowing is okay, for we might not yet be prepared for what is to come. That's why God wants us to trust Him, to wait on His timing, knowing He has already seen what's ahead and will prepare us for whatever lies there. Anything we lack, He'll be more than happy to provide.

Thus, we need not lose sleep over the decisions others may make or the actions others may take, because God's Word tells us, "The fear of man brings a snare, but whoever leans on, trusts in, and puts his confidence in the Lord is safe and set on high" (Proverbs 29:25 AMPC). Remember, *God* is the one in control of *everything* and *everyone*.

Nor do we need to be afraid of the dark. God knows what is hidden there. He'll help us navigate the terrain, seen and unseen. He'll shine His light on whatever He wants us to see—and give us the wisdom we need to understand what He is showing us and where He wants to lead us. All other matters still beyond our ken are left in His hands and under His power. All we have to do is trust Him, remembering that God, the Most High, is the one who holds our right hand (Isaiah 41:13) like a parent holds his or her child's hand, firmly, with no chance of unlinking.

The Ancient of Days (Daniel 7:9, 13, 22) has been around forever. No matter how old you are, God still loves you and sees you as His child and is willing to continue to carry you (Isaiah 46:4), just like He always has (Isaiah 63:9). He'll even send His angels to lift you up so you won't stumble (Psalm 91:11–12).

The way You care for me, Lord, is amazing. Thank You for holding my hand, for being my light in the dark. Amen.

The Power of Prayer

Then the king said to me, "What would you request?" So I prayed to the God of heaven. I said to the king, "If it please the king, and if your servant has found favor before you, send me to Judah, to the city of my fathers' tombs, that I may rebuild it."

NEHEMIAH 2:4–5 NASB

There are times when you need to pray long, lance-like prayers to God and other times when you need short arrow prayers. One man used both methods to great effect.

Nehemiah was a cupbearer, a high-level and trustworthy position, to King Artaxerxes of Persia. When Nehemiah heard that the Jews who'd survived the captivity were in great distress because the walls and gates of Jerusalem were in disrepair, his heart became very heavy, so heavy that he says he "sat down and wept and mourned for days; and I was fasting and praying before the God of heaven" (Nehemiah 1:4 NASB).

Nehemiah then praised God, reminding Him of His promise to His people. He asked God to open His ears and His eyes to Nehemiah's words, as he had been praying to God day and night. Nehemiah admitted to the wrongdoing of God's people. He wisely prayed based on who God is and what He had done, not on who he was and what he'd done. Then Nehemiah prayed God's promises back to Him, reminding Him first of what had already happened (the scattering) and then of the promise that was to follow (the regathering), saying: "Remember the word which You commanded Your servant Moses, saying, 'If you are unfaithful I will scatter you among the peoples; but if you return to Me and keep My commandments and do them. . .I will gather them from there and will bring them to the place where I have chosen to cause My name to dwell' " (Nehemiah 1:8–9 NASB). Nehemiah then asked God for success in addressing the king about Jerusalem's crumbling. Having fasted and prayed lengthy prayers to God over days, he was finally ready to approach King Artaxerxes.

Bringing wine before the king, Nehemiah looked so sorrowful that Artaxerxes asked him what was wrong. This was a make-or-break moment for Nehemiah. He needed his king's help and approval. His hopes and dreams for Jerusalem hinged on Artaxerxes' response. Thus, before allowing one word to cross his lips, Nehemiah silently "prayed to the God of heaven." At the end he obtained not only the king's blessing but his money and equipment to rebuild the wall of Jerusalem!

Prayers are one of the most powerful tools with which God has blessed you. Use them—lances or arrows—well and effectively, and God will reward you.

Lord, loving Master and Creator, open Your ears and eyes as I come humbly before You in prayer. Amen.

Breathing Free and Easy

God, the one and only—I'll wait as long as he says. Everything I need comes from him, so why not? He's solid rock under my feet, breathing room for my soul, an impregnable castle: I'm set for life.

PSALM 62:1–2 MSG

What does waiting on the Lord look like for you? Are you bowing to God's wisdom, calmly, faithfully, and patiently waiting on Him, just like David, writer of the words above? Or are you looking at your circumstances, trying to figure things out on your own? After all, God might not really understand what's happening in your life. Right?

Woman of the Way, the Lord doesn't want you running ahead of Him and His plans for you. No matter what's happening, He wants you to wait for His direction, standing firmly upon Him, breathing free and easy while shielded within His impenetrable fortress.

The people and circumstances plaguing David are revealed in verses 3–4 (MSG): "How long will you gang up on me? How long will you run with the bullies? There's nothing to you, any of you—rotten floorboards, worm-eaten rafters, anthills plotting to bring down mountains, far gone in make-believe. You talk a good line, but every 'blessing' breathes a curse." Obviously, David is not hoodwinked by the people against him.

Yet David is not yet taking any action on his own. Instead, he repeats verses 1–2 to himself: "God, the one and only—I'll wait as long as he says. Everything I hope for comes from him, so why not? He's solid rock under my feet, breathing room for my soul, an impregnable castle: I'm set for life" (verses 5–6 MSG). David clearly knows what God expects him to do and why.

Then David reveals where his hope and glory lie—in God. Why? Because God is "granite-strength and safe-harbor" (verse 7 MSG). He is the only one in whom people can trust *absolutely*. He is the only one for whom they can lay their lives on the line. He is the safest place to be.

David knows that when it comes to humans—they're nothing compared to the Lord (verse 9). They cannot be trusted, nor can a sudden influx of wealth. Besides, "God said this once and for all; how many times have I heard it repeated? 'Strength comes straight from God' " (verse 11 MSG).

Be as this believer. Follow the one you can trust absolutely: God. Put your hope in Him alone, knowing that humans and "dumb luck" cannot be trusted like the solid and eternal rock called the Lord.

You are the source of all I hope for, Lord. Help me keep my eyes on You alone. For You alone are the solid rock beneath my feet. You give my soul room to breathe. With You in my life, I'm set for eternity! Amen.

Peace and Comfort

"The Helper, the Holy Spirit, whom the Father will send in my name, he will teach you all things and bring to your remembrance all that I have said to you. Peace I leave with you; my peace I give to you. Not as the world gives do I give to you. Let not your hearts be troubled, neither let them be afraid."

JOHN 14:26–27 ESV

You have three divine presences to help you as you walk God's road: the Holy Spirit (John 14:15–17), Jesus the Son (John 14:18–21), and God the Father (John 14:22–24). Just before Jesus departed this mortal coil, He told His followers that when He left, the Father would send someone to them, a Spirit who would teach them everything they needed to know to continue in the way of God.

So who is this Holy Spirit? In the Amplified Bible's Classic Edition, seven names are used to describe who and what He represents. The "Comforter" is also called the "Counselor, Helper, Intercessor, Advocate, Strengthener, Standby" (John 14:26). That same Spirit in all His names and forms is here for all who hear the truth and put their trust in God. In fact, "God marked you by giving you His Holy Spirit as a promise. . . . We will receive everything God has for us" (Ephesians 1:13–14 NLV). But how long will He stay with us? "Until God finishes His work of making us complete" (Ephesians 1:14 NLV).

Just after comforting His followers with the knowledge that the Holy Spirit would be here for them while He wasn't, Jesus told them He would leave His peace behind. This peace was left so that the hearts of believers wouldn't be afraid or troubled by the things they'd see in this world. Jesus told His followers, "Stop allowing yourselves to be agitated and disturbed; and do not permit yourselves to be fearful and intimidated and cowardly and unsettled" (John 14:27 AMPC). In other words, you, as a believer, now have access to Jesus' amazing and all-filling peace. He has left it behind—just for you! But have you taken His peace into your heart and really claimed it as your own?

Jesus' peace is beyond all comprehension (Philippians 4:7). But you don't have to understand it to tap into it. All you have to do is cry out to Him, and it's yours for the taking. For Jesus knows your circumstances and has promised to sustain you, strengthen you, and allow His Helper to assist you every which way He can.

Holy Spirit, my Comforter and Helper,
help my heart be calm as I claim and tap into the
peace of Jesus in whose name I pray. Amen.

Encouraged and Strengthened

David was greatly distressed, for the men spoke of stoning him because the souls of them all were bitterly grieved, each man for his sons and daughters. But David encouraged and strengthened himself in the Lord his God. . . . And David inquired of the Lord.

1 SAMUEL 30:6, 8 AMPC

Where do you go, what do you do, how do you hold it together when your world is falling apart? Do you run to a well-loved family member or friend? Do you begin binge eating, indulging in movie marathons, or self-medicating? Or do you go to God, pour out your heart before Him, and ask Him for advice?

David was still on the run from King Saul. He'd been hanging with Achish, a commander of the Philistines. But Achish's fellow commanders wanted David, who had reputedly killed tens of thousands of their Philistine comrades-in-arms, gone. So David and his men went home to Ziklag. That's when they discovered that the Amalekites had not only raided the men's homes and burned down their town but had taken with them their wives and children.

David and his men wailed and wept "until they had no more strength to weep" (1 Samuel 30:4 AMPC). Bitter and heartbroken, the men were so distraught they began talking about stoning David. "But David encouraged and strengthened himself in the Lord his God" (1 Samuel 30:6 AMPC). He then asked God what he should do next. Should he run after the Amalekites? And if he did, should he overtake them and recover all he and his men had lost? God said yes.

So David went, taking six hundred men with him. By the time they arrived at the brook Besor, two hundred of those men were too exhausted to continue. So David went on with the four hundred remaining. In the end, he killed all the Amalekites except four hundred youths who got away on camels. David and his men not only recovered everything that had been taken, including their wives and children, but also captured all the enemy's flocks and herds.

When your life has been turned upside down, go to God and His Word. There you will be given the comfort and encouragement you need. You will receive wisdom for how to go on and how to get things righted as well as the strength to do both. Relying on God and His Word alone, you won't just get back what you lost but will gain even more besides.

Lord, You know what's happening in my life. So I come to You. I search Your Word; I seek Your face. Lift my heart. Give me the encouragement and strength to do what You would have me do, to go where You would have me go. I leave all in Your hands alone. Amen.

A Great Calm

He awoke and rebuked the wind and said to the sea, "Peace! Be still!" And the wind ceased, and there was a great calm.

Mark 4:39 ESV

When you do what you think God wants you to do then later find yourself in a mess of trouble, suffering unforeseen consequences, what do you do? Do you rant and rail against God, accusing Him of not loving you? Do you blame Him for the situation you're in? Do you begin to doubt His direction and start to rely on your own wisdom?

Imagine hanging out with Jesus all day. He tells stories to crowds, teaching them by using imagery from their own lives and society. Later He takes you and your friends aside and clears up any confusion you may have.

As evening begins to fall and you're standing upon the shore, Jesus tells you and the others, "Let us go over to the other side" (Mark 4:35 NASB). Why not? You're with the miracle maker. Everything should be safe and sound if He's telling you to do it. So all thirteen of you—some of whom are seasoned fishermen—pile into the boat. Jesus heads for the stern. Having had a busy day, He soon falls asleep on a cushion.

The next thing you know, a fierce gale rises. The waves are massive! Before you know it, the boat is filling up with water! You decide to wake Jesus. After all, this was *His* idea, not yours.

Frustrated, afraid, and a bit confused, you shake the sleeping Jesus' shoulder, waking Him. The first words out of your mouth as you shout over the wind and waves are, "Master, do You not care that we are perishing?" (Mark 4:38 AMPC). You might as well have asked Him, "Don't You love us, Jesus?"

In response, Jesus "arose and rebuked the wind and said to the sea, Hush now! Be still (muzzled)! And the wind ceased (sank to rest as if exhausted by its beating) and there was [immediately] a great calm (a perfect peacefulness)" (Mark 4:39 AMPC). Then this miracle man turns to you and your fellow followers and says, "Why are you so afraid? Have you still no faith?" (Mark 4:40 ESV).

How many times have you, amid fears and troubles, done the same as these disciples, accusing Jesus of not caring about you? And yet He still saves you, even amid your doubts, tears, and confusion.

Woman of God, remember who Jesus is. He's the one who can calm not only the waves but also your troubled mind and spirit. He's the one who loves you "to the last and to the highest degree" (John 13:1 AMPC). Amid your storms, remember who has sworn never to leave you: the one in the boat with you. No matter how huge your hurricane, be confident Jesus can calm your storm within and without with only two words: "Be still." And peace will reign.

Lord, calm the storm of fears within my soul. Amen.

Go Ahead—Snuggle

His banner over me was love [for love waved as a protecting and comforting banner over my head when I was near him]. . . . [I can feel] his left hand under my head and his right hand embraces me!
Song of Solomon 2:4, 6 AMPC

Where do you turn when you have an overwhelming desire to snuggle up and hold someone close? Perhaps you have a spouse whose arms are always open to your embrace. Maybe you look for that closeness from your mom, dad, or a beloved sibling. Perhaps you reach out for a friend. Or maybe you reach out for a stuffed animal you first had as a child. Therapist Margaret Van Ackeren is quoted as saying, "In most instances, adults sleep with childhood stuffed animals because it brings them a sense of security and reduces negative feelings, such as loneliness and anxiety."[1] Amazingly enough, a 2017 survey found that four out of ten adult Americans still sleep with a teddy bear![2]

When you need comfort, cuddling loved ones or stuffed animals might be good options, but there may be an even better one. Why not just snuggle up to God? After all, He loves you even more than your parents, siblings, and friends. And let's face it, do you really believe your teddy loves you back? The Song of Solomon is a great book to get you in the snuggling-with-God frame of mind. Within its pages is a wonderfully beautiful love poem written by King Solomon to his bride. In its words, you get a sense of the divine love God has for you. You begin to understand and know that no matter what is going on within you or around you, you can enter the presence of your loving shepherd with a heart brimming with love and needful of His peace, His beauty, His presence.

The closer you are to this loving God of yours, the greater the comfort, protection, and peace you will experience in your sleeping and waking hours. Right now, in this moment, imagine lying beside your beloved. Feel His left hand beneath your head, His right hand embracing you, holding you close, shielding you from any danger.

Imagine God speaking to you, saying, "Rise up, my love, my fair one, and come away" (Song of Solomon 2:10 AMPC). Follow Him in your heart, mind, and soul. And when He says, "Let me see your face, let me hear your voice; for your voice is sweet, and your face is lovely" (Song of Solomon 2:14 AMPC), tell Him all that's on your mind, all that burdens your heart. And allow Him to heal you of your worries, fears, troubles. Allow all your questions to fade away, knowing He alone is your answer, your path, your peace, and your joy. Now and forever.

In this moment, Lord, I come to You, desiring Your presence, Your peace. Hold me close. Love me. Lead me. Amen.

The Many Names of God

"Don't be afraid, because I am with you. Don't be intimidated; I am your Elohim. I will strengthen you. I will help you. I will support you with my victorious right hand."

Isaiah 41:10 GW

When you're in a funk that you can't seem to get out of, when you don't know how you're going to make ends meet, when it looks as if the world is crashing down around you, stop. Take a nice deep breath and meditate on how through His many names God has revealed Himself to you in the past, is revealing Himself to you in the present, and will reveal Himself to you in the future.

Ann Spangler, general editor of the Names of God Bible, points out that in Bible times, names were used differently than they are today. While they served to distinguish one person from another and linked people to their families, names also served to share something about a person's character. This couldn't be more true when considering the myriad names of God listed in scripture.

In the beginning of the Bible, God the Creator's name is *Elohim*. If you are an obedient follower and believer of God, Elohim will bless you and everything you do (Deuteronomy 28:2–6, 8). Elohim is also the name of God you can call on when you need strength and courage (Isaiah 41:10).

Yahweh is the name of God that pertains to His always being with you—no matter where you go within or without—and His intervention in worldly events on your behalf. So if you feel lonely, abandoned, or heartbroken, pray to Yahweh, who will not just be your confidence (Proverbs 3:26) but also save you when you are crushed in spirit (Psalm 34:18).

Yahweh Tsebaoth is the name of God that pertains to Him as Lord Almighty, the Lord of armies, and the Lord of hosts. This part of God's character tells you to let go of all you're worried about because He is with you (Psalm 46:10–11). And if you return to Him, He will return to you (Zechariah 1:3).

All these different names of God, as well as all the many names of Jesus (Prince of Peace, light, love, friend, Emmanuel, Master, Son of Man, Son of God) and the names of God's Spirit (Ruach Elohim [Spirit of God], Ruach Hakman [Spirit of Wisdom], Spirit of Christ, Spirit of Truth, Comforter), provide insight into the many ways God interacts with you, is there for you, and blesses you. So when you need help, love, provision, or an intimate conversation, go to the God who meets your every need and longs to hear your voice.

Here I am, Lord. Hear my prayer; heed my plea. Dear Yahweh, Master, and Comforter, be with me as I lift my voice and praise to You. Amen.

The Power of Thoughts

As he thinks in his heart, so is he.
PROVERBS 23:7 AMPC

The Bible tells you that whatever you think in your heart, that's how you'll feel and act. That gives you some idea of how powerful your thought life is!

What you're thinking will cause you to feel a certain way. That feeling will then prompt you to act in a particular way. And that action you take will lead to some sort of result. That's a remarkable chain reaction between your thoughts, feelings, and actions. For example, thoughts of fear may lead you to become fearful. Your feeling fearful may then prompt you to run off, with who knows what kind of results!

No need to worry, though. God has a plan, a strategy for you to follow. But a lot of His strategies depend on your participation—your willingness to work with Him and your trust in Him and His Word.

So how do you get unhelpful thoughts out of your head? The apostle Paul tells you to "be constantly renewed in the spirit of your mind [having a fresh mental and spiritual attitude], and put on the new nature (the regenerate self) created in God's image, [Godlike] in true righteousness and holiness" (Ephesians 4:23–24 AMPC). To get a fresh attitude, one that will move you in the right direction, you have to consciously, moment by moment, choose to depend on the Spirit to make you more and more like Christ.

At first, that idea, of being more like Christ, may put you

off, for you don't want to lose yourself, your personality. But that's not how this works. What happens is that the more you allow Christ to rule your mind and spirit, the more you become *more* yourself, who you truly are, who God made you to be.

You see, God doesn't want you to be like or live like today's culture. He wants you to be different. To be transformed, changed: "Don't become like the people of this world. Instead, change the way you think" (Romans 12:2 GW). Why? So that "you will always be able to determine what God really wants—what is good, pleasing, and perfect" (Romans 12:2 GW) in His eyes, not the eyes of the world.

Wondering how you'll ever discern what God really wants and get the benefits that come with having such knowledge? Good question. Even the prophet Isaiah asked, "Is there anyone around who knows God's Spirit, anyone who knows what he is doing?" (1 Corinthians 2:16 MSG). Fortunately, this question "has been answered: Christ knows, and we have Christ's Spirit" (1 Corinthians 2:16 MSG).

Lord, help me monitor and, when needed, change my thoughts so I will know and receive the benefits that come with Your way of thinking. In Jesus' name I pray, amen.

One Giant Story, Six Powerful Lessons: Part 1

"God, who delivered me from the teeth of the lion and the claws of the bear, will deliver me from this Philistine."
1 Samuel 17:37 MSG

When Saul was king, the Philistine army was encamped at Socoh in Judah. The Philistines stood on a hill on one side. Saul and his men stood on the other. The Valley of Elah lay between them.

The Philistines' giant Goliath came out to taunt the Israelites. Around ten feet tall, he was decked out in bronze armor weighing about 125 pounds. He even had a bronze spear and sword. Goliath dared the Israelites to pick their best warrior and send him out to battle the giant. If Goliath won, the Israelites would become the Philistines' servants. If Goliath lost, the Philistines would become the Israelites' servants.

Goliath's dare struck fear in the hearts of Saul and his men. That's when God's seemingly illogical solution—a shepherd boy named David—walked onto the scene.

David, usually employed in watching his father's sheep, had been sent by his father to check on his three eldest sons who were in Saul's army. While David was in conversation with his brothers, Goliath came out as he had each morning and evening for the past forty days and taunted the Israelites with his battle proposal.

David asked his fellow Israelites, "What's in it for the man who kills that Philistine and gets rid of this ugly blot on Israel's honor?" (1 Samuel 17:26 MSG). The men responded, "The man who kills the giant will have it made. The king will give him a huge reward, offer his daughter as a bride, and give his entire family a free ride" (1 Samuel 17:25 MSG).

David's eldest brother had another suggestion: "Why don't you go home and mind the sheep and your own business instead of hanging around here, waiting to see a bloody battle!" But David ignored his brother's words of discouragement.

Lesson 1: *You need not allow the disheartening words of others to keep you from doing what God calls you to do.* Instead, you can turn away, knowing God will help you.

Lesson 2: *When you're skilled in counting on God, you can more easily rise above your fears.* Are you skilled in that endeavor?

Lord, help me let the discouraging words of others slide off me. Then give me the courage to rise above my fears, depending on You to deliver me. Amen.

One Giant Story, Six Powerful Lessons: Part 2

David took his shepherd's staff, selected five smooth stones from the brook, and put them in the pocket of his shepherd's pack, and with his sling in his hand approached Goliath.

1 SAMUEL 17:40 MSG

In part 1 of the "One Giant Story, Six Powerful Lessons," David had determined to face Goliath on the battlefield, knowing God would deliver him as He had so many times before. And now we see Saul praying for God to help David then trying to dress the boy in a soldier's armor. But once David was outfitted in a soldier's helmet, a coat of mail, and a sword, he couldn't take one step forward. He told Saul, "I can't even move with all this stuff on me. I'm not used to this" (1 Samuel 17:39 MSG). So David removed the soldier's garb. Then he picked up his shepherd's staff, chose five smooth stones from the brook, and put the stones in his shepherd's bag. With sling in hand, David was ready to approach Goliath. For he could do so only with the tools with which God had already trained him.

Lesson 3: *Whatever you're about to face, God has already fully equipped you.* And if you do need anything else, He'll supply it the moment you require it.

Lesson 4: *Be comfortable with who you are, never underestimating who you are and what you can do in God's will and power.*

Now David, as equipped as God would have him, moved toward the Philistine. The giant took one look at the youth and began mocking him, calling him out, ready to make roadkill out of the boy. But the undeterred David told Goliath, "You come at me with sword and spear and battle-ax. I come at you in the name of GOD-of-the-Angel-Armies, the God of Israel's troops, whom you curse and mock. This very day GOD is handing you over to me" (1 Samuel 17:45–46 MSG). And when the battle that belonged to God was over, it was Goliath who lay dead, headless to boot!

God had chosen a young shepherd boy with no battle experience to take down a giant bully, one who'd been warring since before David was born. Yet when David stepped up to the challenge, God delivered him.

Lesson 5: *God's solutions often defy human logic.* For He loves to show people how His power moves through them to give them victory.

Lesson 6: *With God, it's possible for you to do the impossible.* Be firm in your belief that if God is on your side, you *will* slay your own giants.

Lord, thank You for equipping me to do Your will. Help me to be comfortable in my own skin as I step forward in Your name, knowing You will give me victory because You are on my side! Amen.

Never Shaken

I have set the Lord *always before me; because he is at my right hand, I shall not be shaken. Therefore my heart is glad, and my whole being rejoices; my flesh also dwells secure. For you will not abandon my soul to Sheol, or let your holy one see corruption.*

Psalm 16:8–10 ESV

A lot of humorous pictures, silly or snarky cartoons, captioned photos, funny rhyming schemes, and pithy comments made their way around the internet during the recent pandemic. Most times those images, puns, poems, and sayings were welcomed as a momentary relief amid confusing, difficult, and frightening days. Yet sometimes such pieces could stop readers in their tracks. This was one of them:

Coronavirus: Everybody stay inside.
Earthquake: Everybody run outside.
God: "You put the scared people in,
You put the scared people out,
You put the scared people in
And you shake them all about."

To appreciate the humor here, one needs to realize the text attributable to God is a play on the words to the "Hokey Pokey" song, which begins, "You put your right foot in / You take your right foot out / You put your right foot in / And you shake it all about."

As funny as this snippet is, it's a fallacy for believers who put God first and keep Him close by their side. Because of His nearness in their spirits, souls, and minds, they will *never* be shaken! Because they trust in the Lord, they need not allow themselves to become unsettled—no matter what happens in their lives! And because they have a firm foundation, they'll experience the joy that makes their hearts glad.

Trusting believers stick close to God and His Word. They can say to God, "Now you've got my feet on the life path, all radiant from the shining of your face. Ever since you took my hand, I'm on the right way" (Psalm 16:11 MSG).

This truth of being secure in God, so secure that you will never be shaken, is confirmed many ways in God's Word. The believer can say or pray back to God, "Your name, Lord, is a strong tower; a woman right with You can run into it and she will be safe" (Proverbs 18:10, author's paraphrase). A woman in the strong tower of God's name knows that in God she will have strength through Christ who empowers her (Philippians 4:13, author's paraphrase)!

Today and every day, remind yourself that because the Lord your rock, salvation, and fortress is always with you, you will not be shaken (Acts 2:25).

Lord, when the world seems to be crashing down around me, help me remember who You are— my rock, salvation, and fortress. Because You are close to me, I know I will never be shaken, nor stirred. Instead, I will find my joy and security in You. Amen.

Forging New Paths

As a father shows compassion to his children,
so the LORD shows compassion to those who fear him.
PSALM 103:13 ESV

When you find yourself at a dead end to the path you were on, what do you do? Change your trajectory? Start over? Stay where you are, continually kicking yourself for heading down this road in the first place? Go to God and grovelingly ask for a second chance? These are difficult questions when one's mind is more focused on the worldly aftereffects of wrong turns than on God's compassion and understanding.

The prodigal son was in such a situation. As the story goes, a man had two sons. The younger wanted his part of his father's inheritance before his father passed. So the dad divided all he had between his sons. And off went the younger with his chunk of the change.

Far away in another country, the son lived extravagantly and soon had no money left. Hungry, he got a job taking care of pigs. Just as he was about to eat the pigs' feed, he "came to himself" (Luke 15:17 ESV), realizing how foolish he'd been. Deciding that working for his father would keep his belly a lot fuller than taking care of a stranger's pigs, the son decided to go home and tell his father, "Dad, I've screwed up. I'm not worthy to be your son. So please hire me to work for you."

So the younger son headed home, practicing his speech to his father along the way. While he was still a long way off, his father saw him coming. Filled with love and compassion, he ran to his son and began hugging and kissing him! The son began his speech, but the father ignored his words. Instead, he called for his servants to bring the best robe, a ring, and shoes to put on his son—then to kill the fatted calf and cook it for a celebratory dinner because the son who'd been lost had been found!

Just as the prodigal son's father had compassion on his once-wayward son, so does God have compassion on you. He hates to see people continually kicking themselves for wrong turns. Instead, God wants them to run back to Him!

So when you find yourself at a dead end to the path you were on, go to God. There you'll find all the compassion you need. There you'll see a Father so excited to hold you once more that the memory of your misstep (but hopefully not the lesson learned) will fade away and a new path will be forged for you.

Thank You, Lord, for loving me as You do, for forgiving me, for accepting me when I'm finding it hard to love, forgive, and accept myself. As I rush into Your arms, hold me close. Help me find a new way to live, in and through You. Amen.

Nothing at All

Behold, all who are incensed against you shall be put to shame and confounded; those who strive against you shall be as nothing and shall perish. You shall seek those who contend with you, but you shall not find them; those who war against you shall be as nothing at all.

ISAIAH 41:11–12 ESV

God makes a bold promise to His followers, telling them that those who come against them, those who are angry with them, will be shamed and confused. Their contenders will become as nothing and die off. In other words, the enemies of God's people won't have the power, strength, or ability to harm them!

God had already proved He could accomplish such a feat when the Egyptians came to chase down the Israelites and bring them back to serve as slaves. As God's people stood between the waters and Pharaoh's army, Moses encouraged them by saying, "Fear not; stand still (firm, confident, undismayed) and see the salvation of the Lord which He will work for you today. For the Egyptians you have seen today you shall never see again. The Lord will fight for you, and you shall hold your peace and remain at rest" (Exodus 14:13–14 AMPC).

After the people heard Moses' words, the angel of God and the pillar of cloud that had been leading the Israelites moved to their rear, putting a buffer between them and the Egyptians. Moses then stretched out his hand over the sea and God drove the waters back so the Israelites could cross the Red Sea on dry ground. When the Egyptian forces who'd followed them tried to catch up with them in the midst of the sea, the waters crashed over them and they drowned. Just as God had promised, the Israelites never again saw Pharaoh, his forces, his chariots, or his horses.

When you feel embattled, unsure of your strength, power, and footing, listen to God telling you, "Fear not, for I am with you; be not dismayed, for I am your God; I will strengthen you, I will help you, I will uphold you with my righteous right hand" (Isaiah 41:10 ESV).

Be assured that whatever has come against you will at some point never be seen again. It will be like the Egyptian forces, overwhelmed by the power of the one who not only holds your right hand but holds you *in* His hand. He's the one who says, "Fear not, I am the one who helps you" (Isaiah 41:13 ESV).

Lord, when my back is up against the wall, when I have no strength left, help me be bold. Help me look to You for salvation. Give me the confidence I need, Lord, to stand my ground, to hold my peace, to stay calm while You vanquish those against me so that I will never see them again. To You I look and pray, amen.

Spiritual Eyesight

Fear not; for those with us are more than those with them. Then Elisha prayed, Lord, I pray You, open his eyes that he may see. And the Lord opened the young man's eyes, and he saw, and behold, the mountain was full of horses and chariots of fire round about Elisha.

2 Kings 6:16–17 AMPC

At war with Israel, the king of Syria would consult with his military officers then tell them where he'd want an ambush set. As if he were in the next room next to where the Syrians were plotting their attacks, the prophet Elisha would send word to the king of Israel, telling him the site where their enemy would be ambushing the Israelite forces. It happened over and over again. So furious was the Syrian king that he finally decided to send "horses, chariots, and a great army" (2 Kings 6:14 AMPC) to surround Dothan, the city where Elisha lived, at night.

The next morning, Elisha's servant went out early. To his astonishment and fear, he saw the Syrian army with their horses and chariots surrounding Dothan. The servant asked Elisha what they should do. Elisha told his servant to stay calm. That the forces *with* him and Elisha were much greater than the ones *against* them.

When Elisha prayed to ask God to open his servant's eyes, the Lord did so. The young man was then able to see a mountain full of horses and chariots of fire around himself and his master!

As the Syrians made their way closer to Elisha, he prayed once more, asking God, "Please strike this people with blindness"

(2 Kings 6:18 ESV), and God did. In this way, Elisha was able to redirect the enemy army out of the city and lead them to Samaria. There Elisha prayed for the men's eyes to be opened. How shocked the Syrians must have been to find themselves standing in the center of enemy territory!

Elisha instructed the king of Israel to feed the Syrians and send them home. For a while after this, "the bands of Syria came no more into the land of Israel" (2 Kings 6:23 AMPC).

Sometimes our vision is limited. We see only what is against us, which we consider "reality." But there is another way of seeing what's truly before you. When you think there's no way out of a situation, take your concerns to God. Ask Him to show you the true reality of your circumstances. As you trust Him more and more, you will begin to see things from God's perspective. You'll see beyond your own limited point of view and see God's reality—and more besides.

Lord, open my eyes to Your reality as I trust in You more and more each day. Amen.

Well-Placed Confidence

The Lord is on my side and takes my part, He is among those who help me. . . . It is better to trust and take refuge in the Lord than to put confidence in man. It is better to trust and take refuge in the Lord than to put confidence in princes.

PSALM 118:7–9 AMPC

Sometimes people are hard to trust. Your best friend may promise to keep your secret; next thing you know, you discover from another friend that your bestie has actually betrayed your confidence. When you confront her later, she may try to laugh it off. When that doesn't work, she might apologize. . . But you may never trust her again.

The same holds true with work partners, spouses, boyfriends, and relatives—even your kids and parents! People often can let you down. Why? Because they're people. And people are not perfect. In fact, you might say they are downright unreliable. Just ask God. He could probably give you an earful on that subject, beginning with the garden back in Eden.

No matter what people may say or promise, you'll sometimes find them doing the opposite. Some more than others. Although you may not be able to trust any other *human*, there is someone you can trust: God.

When you're right with God, you can bet He'll be on your side. He'll take your part in any argument or skirmish. Why? Because once you commit yourself—body, soul, spirit, and mind—to Him, He will turn Himself inside out to help you.

At times, you may find it difficult to trust God because so

many humans have let you down. Also, it may be hard to have faith in an invisible supernatural force like God when you can see the force and power of a human being right in front of you. But let's be clear: God, although invisible (for the most part), is so much more powerful than any other entity—animal, vegetable, mineral, or spiritual. He's the God "Whose power no foe can withstand" (Psalm 91:1 AMPC)!

So the next time you're in a pickle, go to God before you go anywhere else. You'll find He will not just answer you but set you down in a safe and wide-open space where you can catch your breath. With God right next to you, no human can harm you! With God working His will in your situation, you can be sure He'll *become* your salvation, your deliverer. And you'll soon be praising God for what He has accomplished.

You amaze me, Lord. Help me be as faithful and committed to You as You are to me. Remind me to turn to You first when I need a friend. For You truly are the best friend a woman can ever have. In Jesus' name, amen!

Early Seekers

I love those who love me, and those who seek me early and diligently shall find me.
Proverbs 8:17 AMPC

If you ever begin to wonder where God is, consider asking yourself where *you've* been. For when you feel as if God has vacated the premises, isn't listening, or has faded out of your life, chances are that you are the one who has cut and run. That you are the one who has left God hanging, stopped paying attention to His calls and whispers, or exited the spiritual scene.

God *loves* those who seek Him diligently (in all His aspects) and who do such seeking early—before the busyness or business of the day crowds Him out of your heart and mind. God *wants* to be and *insists* on being your foundation, an important and integral part of your life, not someone you visit only when you're desperate or need something. God wants a daily conversation time with you. You know, the kind where you speak while He listens, and then He speaks while you listen. And He wants you doing it early, just as Jesus did: "In the morning, long before daylight, He got up and went out to a deserted place, and there He prayed" (Mark 1:35 AMPC).

And God wants you seeking Him—His face, His wisdom, His advice, His help—with an attitude and approach like David's when he was in the wilderness: "O God, you are my God; earnestly I seek you; my soul thirsts for you; my flesh faints for you, as in a dry and weary land where there is no water" (Psalm 63:1 ESV).

Moses told the Israelites that the Lord wanted their coming to Him every day to become a necessity—as if they couldn't start their day without Him—and that they should do so intentionally and intensely, saying, "You will seek the LORD your God and you will find him, if you search after him with all your heart and with all your soul" (Deuteronomy 4:29 ESV). Notice the *if* in that sentence. You will seek and then find God *if* you do so with your entire heart and soul. In other words, you must take seeking God seriously; you must not go to Him with a halfhearted attitude but with real purpose. Speaking through the prophet Jeremiah, God told His exiled people the same thing, saying: "When you come looking for me, you'll find me. Yes, when you get serious about finding me and want it more than anything else, I'll make sure you won't be disappointed. . . . I'll turn things around for you" (Jeremiah 29:13–14 MSG).

Today, if you haven't already, seek your Lord and Master. Have a good heart-to-heart discussion with Him. And remember the privilege your going after God affords you: "Seek and keep on seeking and you shall find" (Luke 11:9 AMPC).

Here I am, Lord, coming to You before my day starts. Let's talk. Amen.

God Before You and God With You

It is the Lord Who goes before you; He will [march] with you; He will not fail you or let you go or forsake you; [let there be no cowardice or flinching, but] fear not, neither become broken [in spirit—depressed, dismayed, and unnerved with alarm].

Deuteronomy 31:8 AMPC

When you have to take a major step out of your comfort zone, it can be exciting and terrifying at the same time. The challenge is not to let the scary parts of a situation or circumstance keep you from moving forward.

That's not to say there aren't some instances in which you have every right to be frightened. Consider wars, pandemics, terrorism, earthquakes, tornadoes, hurricanes, and so on. Each of those events can scare people out of their wits—and for good reasons. But walkers of the Way cannot let fears (amid those very real dangers) put any kind of dent in their confidence in God.

God's people have, at various times, turned to other countries for help instead of turning to Him. Perhaps they felt it was easier, more logical to put their confidence in a physical mass of armed warriors than to put their trust in the invisible yet powerful supernatural being *who created them*! The problem is that when you trust people, countries, material things, wealth, governments, institutions, or anything else instead of God, there's a very good chance you'll be disappointed. For no one loves you as much or has more power and resources to help you than your God.

God had told the 120-year-old Moses that he wouldn't be crossing over into the Promised Land. Instead, his assistant, Joshua, would be the people's new leader and would take them across the Jordan River. Moses, in his farewell address to Israel, tells God's people that God will be going ahead of them into the Promised Land. He will stick with them the entire time, marching with them as they cross over to the other side. Thus, God's people needn't be afraid, nor become worried or depressed. Instead they should "be strong, courageous, and firm; fear not nor be in terror before them, for it is the Lord your God Who goes with you; He will not fail you or forsake you" (Deuteronomy 31:6 AMPC).

Just as God went before and walked with His Israelites, taking them into the Promised Land, so He goes before and walks with you, taking you into what He has promised you. Thus, no matter how scary things seem, minute by minute you can trust that God has gone before you and is walking with you. So don't fear but stay strong and courageous. God's got you and your situation under control.

Lord, help me remember You are checking things out ahead of me. And You'll be walking with me, no matter where I go. Because of You, I need never fear. Amen.

Praiseworthy

"You have exalted yourself against the Lord of heaven; and they have brought the vessels of His house before you, and. . .have been drinking wine from them; and you have praised the gods of silver and gold, of bronze, iron, wood and stone, which do not see, hear or understand. But the God in whose hand are your life-breath and all your ways, you have not glorified."

DANIEL 5:23 NASB

A Babylonian king named Belshazzar had a feast to which he invited all the nobles of the land. They were drinking wine in the vessels that Belshazzar's predecessor, King Nebuchadnezzar, had brought back from the temple in Jerusalem. To add insult to injury, the revelers made toasts to their own gods while sipping from temple cups!

In response to the Babylonians' misdirected praises, "immediately the fingers of a human hand appeared and wrote on the plaster of the wall of the king's palace, opposite the lampstand. And the king saw the hand as it wrote" (Daniel 5:5 ESV). At that moment, the color drained from the drunken king's face, his heart began racing, his limbs became limp, and his knees knocked together.

When no wise men, magicians, or astrologers could discern the meaning of what the disembodied hand had written, the king's mother suggested the wise dream interpreter named Daniel be called. So Daniel was summoned and came before the king. He was able to interpret not just the message but its meaning: Because King Belshazzar had neither humbled himself nor honored the true God, his days of rule were numbered. As it turned out, so were the days of his life, for Belshazzar was murdered that very same night.

Take some time to pause in this moment and reflect: Do you humble yourself before your God? Do you give Him the glory and honor He deserves or give them to some other person or thing(s)?

Your God—the one "in Whose hand your breath is" (Daniel 5:23 AMPC)—is the one who cradles your very life force. He is the one who not only created but contains, maintains, and sustains everything you see—and don't see—around you. He is the one who made a pathway for you to follow, one on which you can make your way to Him and then live with Him forever and ever. This God is the one to whom you owe everything.

Today, remember who holds you, your life, your soul, your spirit, your body, and your breath in His hand. Praise Him for what He has done, is doing, and will do in your life. Thank Him for walking before, with, and after you. Raise your voice in praise of the true three-in-one God, humbling yourself before Him. For to Him alone, you owe all.

You hold my very breath in Your hand, Lord God. You are my Yahweh, my Abba, my all. I praise, honor, and glorify You! In Jesus' name, amen.

Relax

"What I'm trying to do here is to get you to relax, to not be so preoccupied with getting, so you can respond to God's giving. People who don't know God and the way he works fuss over these things, but you know both God and how he works."
Matthew 6:31–32 MSG

God wants you to relax, to not be so preoccupied with where your next shirt, meal, or paycheck is going to come from. That can be extremely difficult sometimes, especially when it seems as if the entire world has collapsed around you, your loved ones, and your dreams.

When the world you live in snaps back into its old pattern or starts looking like nothing you've ever seen before, you need not worry about God supplying your every—yes, your every—need! How do you know that's true? Because God says so. And God is true to His word.

God is able to bless you above and beyond what you ask for—at all times—so that you can do all the good work He has called you to do (2 Corinthians 9:8). He will open up the very heavens and send rain when you need it; on top of that, He will bless all the work your hands perform (Deuteronomy 28:12).

And God doesn't just deal in the tangibles but in the intangibles. Not only is your Lord compassionate and gracious and slow to anger, but He abounds in love and faithfulness—for those who follow in His wake (Exodus 34:6)! He'll make sure you not only have life but have it to the full (John 10:10).

But you can't just sit on the sidelines while God keeps giving and giving and giving to you. He wants you to give away some of the things with which He gifts you, not hold on to them with a white-knuckled grip (Luke 6:38). So if you see someone who needs a shirt, a little love, a kindness, or some physical help, don't hesitate to act. See what clothing you might give away. Send a card of love and encouragement. Offer to be a friend. Or roll up your sleeves and do for someone what that person cannot do for him- or herself.

As you go about living a life of giving, you'll soon find that what you actually need is less than you thought. And that itself is a gift from God.

Today and every day, remember that God is in the business of providing abundantly for His people (Proverbs 3:10). So stop worrying about what you need. Just relax, knowing God will be sure to pour out what you require and truly desire. All you need to do is continue to walk in His way and help others along *your* way—in Jesus' name.

Lord, I am so thankful You always provide what I need. Please show me who I can bless today. Amen.

God's "Yet"

Bless our God, O peoples; let the sound of his praise be heard, who has kept our soul among the living and has not let our feet slip. For you, O God, have tested us; you have tried us as silver is tried.

Psalm 66:8–10 ESV

When you go through a period of testing, you may not feel as if God has your best interests at heart. But the truth is He does. God may take you through times of trouble and trial, but He will walk with you through them and bring you out a wiser woman, one who is closer to the Lord. In fact, hardships often do more to build your faith than any blessing might.

That's what happened when God brought His people out of Egypt and into the Promised Land. They had to go through quite a lot to get from point A to point B. The psalmist wrote, "You brought us into the net; you laid a crushing burden on our backs; you let men ride over our heads; we went through fire and through water" (Psalm 66:11–12 ESV). But, as in many situations, the psalmist added a "yet" at the end of these verses, writing, "yet you have brought us out to a place of abundance" (verse 12 ESV).

When we need maturing in our faith walk with God, He will be sure to try us and test us, to wake us up to His reality, not that of the current world. For God wants us to understand His desires for us and to realize that He's working according to a plan for our good. He wants us to know that all the world offers us will one day fade away. But God and His followers will remain forever. And for those followers, those who are with Him, God will part seas so that they can follow Him on dry land. But for those who are not with Him, God may open up the earth and have it swallow them. That's why in life you want to be sure to choose the right side: God's side.

When you're on God's side, you're not to harbor any ill will or evil in your heart. For if you do, your own prayers, your own cries, your own entreaties to God may be delayed or hindered at best (Psalm 66:18). But if you fear God and walk faithfully with Him, harboring goodness in your heart, He will not turn away your prayer, nor withhold His loving-kindness from you.

So today, if you feel that God is testing your mettle, consider that He is doing so to help you mature in your faith and form an even deeper connection to Him.

Even through trials, Lord, You are blessing me. Help me to keep that in mind, Lord, so that I look for You and Your silver lining in every cloud that rises above me. In Jesus' name, amen.

Open Windows of Heaven

"Bring the full tithe into the storehouse, that there may be food in my house. And thereby put me to the test, says the Lord *of hosts, if I will not open the windows of heaven for you and pour down for you a blessing until there is no more need."*

Malachi 3:10 ESV

God loves us so much that He pledges to open the windows of heaven and pour out blessings upon us. But a few conditions are attached to this promise.

One condition is that we're to bring our tithes into God's storehouse. In this verse, the word *storehouse* refers to His temple. For us, that means bringing God's portion of our increase into His church. Two other conditions are that we are to make such contributions on a regular basis (1 Corinthians 16:2) and do so joyfully (Matthew 6:1–4; 2 Corinthians 8:1–15).

When it comes to bringing our God-given income and increase back to Him, the Lord would have us be like the Israelites Moses was leading. After He shared the how-to-build-a-temple instructions with the people, they all went back to their tents and "everyone whose heart stirred him, and everyone whose spirit moved him. . .brought the Lord's contribution to be used for the tent of meeting" (Exodus 35:21 ESV).

Everyone with a willing and cheerful heart brought so much that Moses finally had to make a proclamation: "Let no man or woman do anything more for the contribution for the sanctuary" (Exodus 36:6 ESV). Because the people had brought so many more materials than were needed, they had to be "*restrained* from bringing" (verse 6 ESV, emphasis added)!

Those people are the good example. But Jesus cited a not-so-good example in a parable about a rich man who was trying to figure out what to do with his crop. His barn wasn't nearly big enough to store that year's harvest. So he decided to raze his barns and construct bigger ones. Then he said to himself, "Soul, you have many good things put away in your building. It will be all you need for many years to come. Now rest and eat and drink and have lots of fun" (Luke 12:19 NLV). But God had other plans. He called the man a fool and told him, "Tonight your soul will be taken from you. Then who will have all the things you have put away?" (Luke 12:20 NLV).

Which tack will you take when it comes to giving a portion of all God has given you back to Him? Be wise. Test God in giving your tithe with a cheerful heart—and He will be sure to bless you more than you can think or imagine.

To You, Lord, I tithe a portion of my life and my goods—with a willing and cheerful heart. Thank You for all Your blessings, now and forever. Amen.

Hold Tight

A Message from God-of-the-Angel-Armies:
"At that time, ten men speaking a variety of languages
will grab the sleeve of one Jew, hold tight, and say,
'Let us go with you. We've heard that God is with you.' "
Zechariah 8:23 msg

Imagine suffering from a hemorrhage for twelve whole years. Your body has been examined by so many doctors you've lost count. Not to mention all the different remedies you've tried. And now you're not only out of money but worse off than in the beginning. But word has come to you of a man named Jesus. People say He heals them. Suddenly you have hope once more.

You hear Jesus is in town. But so many people are surrounding Him, you wonder how you'll ever make your way through. You push out of your head the fact that, in your condition, you're considered unclean. Instead, you just keep saying to yourself, *If I just touch the hem of His garment, I'll be well once more.*

You make your way through the crowd, come up behind Jesus, and touch His garment, all the while still saying to yourself, *If I just touch the hem of His garment, I'll be well once more.* And in that very nanosecond, the flow of blood within you dries up and you can feel that you are healed!

But you're not in the clear yet. Because it appears Jesus felt that life-healing power leaving His body. Before you can escape through the crowd, He has turned around and asked, "Who touched My clothes?" (Mark 5:30 ampc).

You don't answer. He's still looking for who touched Him.

Now you know you're in for it. You've *got* to come clean. So, trembling, you fall to your knees, weeping, and tell Jesus the entire story.

The next words you hear are etched into your heart and mind. It's His voice saying, "Daughter, you took a risk of faith, and now you're healed and whole. Live well, live blessed! Be healed of your plague" (Mark 5:34 MSG)

What a story! What a Lord! What a Redeemer you have in Jesus! This nameless woman had such amazing faith. Her adherence to her faith in Jesus and His power is what helped her make her way through the crowd. And for that faith she was rewarded more than she'd ever dreamed she'd be!

You too have access to Jesus! You too can, through prayer, reach out and touch His sleeve or the hem of His garment and be healed. Just take that risk of faith. And Jesus will respond, commending your faith, making you whole, and blessing your life.

Jesus, here I am, reaching out for You, extending a hand so that I can touch Your garment. I'm holding on tight. I pray You will make me whole once more! Amen.

Only Keep On Believing

While he was still talking, some people came from the leader's house and told him, "Your daughter is dead. Why bother the Teacher any more?" Jesus overheard what they were talking about and said to the leader, "Don't listen to them; just trust me."

MARK 5:35–36 MSG

Jesus had just exorcised some evil spirits from a man He'd found bound with shackles and wandering around among some tombs. Then He'd angered a bunch of villagers because He'd sent those now-disembodied spirits into a herd of pigs—about two thousand of them—who had then run off a cliff, fallen into the sea, and drowned.

So Jesus went back across the sea. After landing, He faced another crowd of people looking for help. One man, Jairus, was a ruler in the synagogue. Seeing Jesus, he fell down at His feet and begged Him to come lay His hands on his dying daughter, "so that she may be healed and live" (Mark 5:23 AMPC). So Jesus went with him. But the crowd pressed in around Him from all sides. And a woman in the crowd, the one with the issue of blood, reached out to touch His robe, knowing if she did so, she'd be healed. And as she touched Him and *was* healed, Jesus stopped in His tracks, asking who touched Him.

While Jesus was speaking with the woman, some people from Jairus' house told the ruler that his twelve-year-old daughter was dead—so why bother Jesus anymore?

"Overhearing but ignoring what they said, Jesus said to

the ruler of the synagogue, Do not be seized with alarm and struck with fear; only keep on believing" (Mark 5:36 AMPC).

Once at Jairus' house, Jesus allowed no one but Peter, James, and John to enter the home with Him. Seeing and hearing all the people weeping and wailing as they mourned for Jairus' daughter, Jesus said aloud, "Why are you making such a racket? The child is not dead. She's merely sleeping." The weepers and wailers laughed at Jesus, so He had them go outside.

Then Jesus, accompanied by the three disciples and the child's parents, went upstairs. Taking the child by the hand, He said, "Little one, arise." And, amazingly enough, she got up and began walking. Then, before He went on His way, Jesus told the parents to give the girl something to eat.

When you have Jesus in your life, you need never be afraid or alarmed no matter what is happening. Simply follow Jesus' advice: "Only keep on believing." Because when you do, you make room for miracles to happen.

Jesus, thank You for always being here when I need You. No matter what is happening in my life, help me have hope and keep the faith. Help me to simply trust You, to "only keep on believing." In Your name I pray, amen.

Take a Break

The apostles then rendezvoused with Jesus and reported on all that they had done and taught. Jesus said, "Come off by yourselves; let's take a break and get a little rest." For there was constant coming and going. They didn't even have time to eat.

MARK 6:30–31 MSG

We women usually have a lot on our plates. That's partly because we are also often the ones who *clean* the plates. Yet it's not just that our hands are the ones likely to be elbow deep in soap suds. We may also be dealing with children and their sticky fingers. Throw in a husband and his somewhat sloppy habits and perhaps a pet or two or three, and it's a wonder we find time to do anything. Or if we're a little older, we may still be helping take care of a husband and perhaps a pet or two and a grandchild or three or eight.

We may also find ourselves involved (sometimes *over*involved) at church. Chances are we're a Sunday school teacher, member of the worship team, deacon, or VBS coordinator. And then there may be outside organizations vying for our time, whether a favorite charity, an online workout program, or the local volunteer firefighters. You name it, women are involved. The propensity to take on a lot of projects may be part of our genetic makeup. The problem is that sometimes we have trouble balancing all our activities; we may even have trouble making time for God!

Here's the good news: Jesus loves that we are involved, looking after our families, our churches, our bodies, and our outside interests. But there is a limit to our time and our energy. Jesus knows how tired and wrung out we can become—because usually the last person we take care of is ourselves.

Jesus has a surefire program that can lead to continual power, peace, and contentment. And it's simple, really. Jesus wants you to get the break you need—physically *and* spiritually.

Let's face it, no one can keep hurrying through life, running from one commitment, task, or person to another, and still stay physically healthy and spiritually grounded. There are times you need a break. And Jesus wants to make sure you get one.

God knows all you are doing. He knows the challenges you may be up against. After all, He's going before you and walking beside you. He knows the road you are on. So when you hear Him say, "Come off by yourselves; let's take a break and get a little rest," follow Him wherever He leads. Sit under a tree, take a long walk, lie down on your bed, or open His Word. Get away with the one who loves you like no other. And allow yourself to rest easy in His arms.

I do need a break, Lord. Let's spend some time alone, resting, sleeping, reading, talking. I'm ready when You are. You name the place and I'll be there! Amen.

Your Good Shepherd

God, my shepherd! I don't need a thing. You have bedded me down in lush meadows, you find me quiet pools to drink from. True to your word, you let me catch my breath and send me in the right direction.

Psalm 23:1–3 MSG

One of the most comforting psalms ever written is Psalm 23. From the first verse to the last, David recounts all the wonderful ways God blesses him as he follows his Lord.

When you put yourself in God's hands, following Him from dawn till dusk, you will want for nothing. He will make you lie down and rest amid His green pastures. He will lead you to still water from which you can drink. And if you are very thirsty, ill, or tired, your good shepherd will cup His hands and bring His sparkling water to your parched lips, reviving you physically, mentally, emotionally, and spiritually while instilling peace within you. He will restore your soul, give you a chance to catch your breath, and then send you off in the right direction.

Even when you walk through those dark valleys, amid the deep, deep darkness of disquiet, danger, depression, desperation, and death, you need not fear. For your shepherd carries a rod and staff to defend, guide, and protect you. But the benefits don't stop there.

Your shepherd serves you an all-you-can-eat dinner in the sight of your enemies. He revives you with His oil. And the cup He gives you spills over with unending blessings, within and without, in this world and the next.

When you walk in the path laid out by your shepherd, when you follow Him determinedly, trusting Him at every bend in the road, at every seeming dead end, He will care for you every step of the way. And His goodness, His kindness, His love, grace, and mercy, will chase you all the days of your life as you dwell in His house, kingdom, and realm.

When you feel anxious, afraid, uncertain, unmotivated, or unwell, remember your good shepherd. See if you have deviated from the path He laid out for you. Seek His face, confirming that He, the Lord, is indeed your shepherd. That to follow Him means you have more blessings than you can count. And you will find yourself exactly where God would have you be once more.

Lord, You are my good shepherd. With You in my heart and life, I lack nothing. For when I follow You, I know I am just where You want me to be. So here I am, Lord—ready to allow You to guide me down Your path of love, joy, and blessing. In Jesus' name, amen.

God's Eternal Love

Though I walk in the midst of trouble, you preserve my life; you stretch out your hand against the wrath of my enemies, and your right hand delivers me.

Psalm 138:7 ESV

In this world, chances are you'll see your share of trouble. But there's an upside, as there always is for God's people. Amid all that trouble, you will get an opportunity to see how God works in your life for your good and for the good of the world.

The writer of Psalm 138 knew how much God had blessed and was still blessing his life. That's why he begins his song by thanking God from the bottom of his heart. Happily singing God's praises, he kneels before Him, bowing down to the ground, lifting up his Lord's many names—provider, counselor, peace, love, Lord, Abba, Almighty. He applauds God's unending love for him and the faithfulness He never ceases to show toward him.

You can follow the same path laid out by this psalmist. Make a list of the many ways God has blessed you in the past hour, day, week, month, year, decade. Praise God for all the ways He has shown up for you—as defender, refuge, fortress, guide, beloved, friend, giver of life, and so on. Or come up with your very own praise name for your Lord.

Make note of how many times you called on God and His answer came swiftly—when there was no hesitation, no delay. When you were in dire straits, seeking direction, waiting for a word, God was there, guiding, helping, teaching. And because of God's answer, because He moved on your behalf, your soul was strengthened. You could not help but see and acknowledge God's power working within you.

Even as you found yourself walking forward but encountering pitfalls along the way, God blessed you by keeping you safe and on track. He stretched out His powerful hand against those who wished you ill. With His other hand He pulled you near, into His arms, away from the fray. So close were you to Him, you could feel the glow of His Spirit, the warmth of His breath, the peace of His presence.

You know that this God will never leave you but continually work in and through you, because He created you for a purpose, one that only you can fulfill in this time, in this place, on this planet. And as He works His will in and through your life, you are certain His love will ever follow you as He continually turns toward you, filling your life with the blessings He prepared thousands of years ago just for you, blessings that are waiting for you in this moment, this day, this life.

Thank You, Lord of my heart, for all You do for, in, with, and through me. Most of all, Lord, thank You for loving me, not just today but forever and ever. Amen.

Peace Every Moment

"Steep your life in God-reality, God-initiative, God-provisions. Don't worry about missing out. You'll find all your everyday human concerns will be met. Give your entire attention to what God is doing right now, and don't get worked up about what may or may not happen tomorrow. God will help you deal with whatever hard things come up when the time comes."

MATTHEW 6:33–34 MSG

You read the morning paper; check out social media; get a call, text, or email from a friend; and watch the evening news. As the days go by, you realize you're having trouble sleeping, eating, even smiling. Why? Because you are a woman who cares about others, who wants to see a world at peace, who can't understand why people keep hurting each other.

You see, the problem here is that you've so steeped yourself in humankind-reality, humankind-initiative, humankind-provisions that you've forgotten what God, His power, and His provisions can do.

God doesn't want you worrying about every little and big thing that happens in your house, church, town, county, state, country, or world. He doesn't want you to worry that you're not as well off as the Joneses. He doesn't want you to think that what you're seeing happening in the world is the true reality. Why? Because it's not.

God is doing things that you, with your limited perspective, cannot see. He's working in the visible and the invisible world. He's working all around you and within you. And He will never stop working, making sure all your needs are more than met.

What God does want you to do is know that He will provide for you. That He will address your every concern—little and big. God wants you to give all your time and attention to Him and what He's doing. He wants you to receive the peace He offers you.

So don't worry about today. And don't worry about tomorrow. When tomorrow comes, God will help you through it, just as He's been doing throughout your life.

To help you start steeping your life in God, consider watching less news. Instead, pick up the Word and see what news or new thing God reveals to you there. Instead of getting on social media, consider taking a nice long walk, in a park or in the countryside if possible. Take any concerns of lack to God in prayer, asking Him to give you peace and perspective. And remember: Tomorrow is another day. God will still be here to help you through whatever comes, be it rain or shine.

I've lost my perspective, Lord. So I'm coming to You to get it back. Help me focus more on You, Your Word, Your truth, Your promises, and Your blessings than on what is happening on this side of heaven. For I know that with You, I never need to worry. You've got this. Amen.

Out of Focus

[Joshua and Caleb said,] "The land, which we passed through to spy it out, is an exceedingly good land. If the LORD delights in us, he will bring us into this land and give it to us, a land that flows with milk and honey. Only do not rebel against the LORD. And do not fear the people of the land. . . . Their protection is removed from them, and the LORD is with us; do not fear them."

NUMBERS 14:7–9 ESV

Now that His people have made it out of Egypt, God tells Moses to have some men (one from each tribe of Israel) go into the Promised Land and check things out. So Moses sends twelve men to spy out the land before them. He gives them specific assignments: Go into the hill country and see what the land is like. Then check out the people to see if they're weak or strong. Estimate how many there are. See how they live, what they grow, etc.

So the twelve spies head into the Promised Land. Forty days later they come back with some fruit to show God's people. Yes, they report, it's a land of milk and honey. *However*, the people living there are strong, their cities fortified and enormous. *And* the people are descendants of giants!

Caleb, one of the twelve spies, tries to interrupt the men, to calm everyone down by focusing on God's perspective, saying, "We can go up there right now and take over this land. Easy."

But ten of the spies disagree. They say the land eats people up. That the natives of the land are much stronger than the Israelites and are massive. "We looked like grasshoppers in our own eyes, and we looked the same to them" (Numbers 13:33 NLV).

Only Joshua and Caleb disagreed with the other ten spies. Only Joshua and Caleb kept their eyes on the omnipotent one rather than the obstacles in front of them. And after forty years of wilderness wandering, Joshua and Caleb would be the only spies blessed to step into the Promised Land.

How horrible to go through life looking at the obstacles in your path as giants you'll never be able to battle, much less subdue, because they see you as tiny and insignificant. Even worse, imagine seeing *yourself* as tiny and insignificant.

Only by believing God's Word, by putting your faith in Him and His promises, can you overcome the challenges life puts in your way and keep yourself on the path to the land God has promised you.

God is with you. So don't fear. Simply walk on, knowing you don't walk alone. For with God, you can be more than brave enough, big enough, and strong enough to enter your own land of promise.

Lord, help me keep my eyes on You, knowing that You can tear down any obstacles standing in my way. Amen.

Your Divine Assignment

May He grant you according to your heart's desire and fulfill all your plans. We will [shout in] triumph at your salvation and victory, and in the name of our God we will set up our banners. May the Lord fulfill all your petitions.

PSALM 20:4–5 AMPC

God has a specific plan, a certain purpose for your life. He has prepared you since the very beginning to play a role in a particular place and at a particular time.

God is the one who shaped you, "first inside, then out" (Psalm 139:13 MSG), while you were still in your mother's womb. It was the Lord who knit you together, cell by cell, bone by bone. It was God's eyes that saw you unformed. He is the one who entered you and your days into the book of life (Psalm 139:16).

Yet it is only when God's purposes and your wants are the same that He will grant you all your heart's desires and help you accomplish all your plans. Then He will send blessings of good to meet you and set a gold crown upon your head (Psalm 21:3). Then He will give you "long life forever and evermore" (Psalm 21:4 AMPC).

Take some time each day to think about your heart's desires. Then go to God and share them with Him. Ask Him to let you know if your wants line up with His wants for you, if your plans run parallel to His plans for your life. If you and God aren't on the same proverbial page, He will definitely let you know. But the crucial part of this entire scenario is your keeping in close contact with the one who knows all. For if you are walking in a way or down a path that is completely different from what God had in mind for you, you may soon find yourself walking alone or meeting more unexpected challenges and roadblocks than usual.

That is why an intimate relationship with your Lord and Savior is crucial. Each and every day, you need to be checking in, sharing your thoughts, feelings, and intuitions with the one who created you and this world according to His grand plan.

In those areas where you are uncertain as to your life path, allow God to lead you into His Word to help you home in on your specific divine assignment. Ask Him to bring people into your life who will help you determine His will and way. Consider your current circumstances and see if any leads can be found there. And at all times, remain steady in prayer, knowing God only wants good for you and can be trusted to help you find and stay on the right road, the one He has already paved for you.

I come to You, Lord, asking for Your divine direction as I seek to find what part You would have me play in Your will and way. Amen.

Look Up

I will lift up my eyes to the hills [around Jerusalem, to sacred Mount Zion and Mount Moriah]— From whence shall my help come? My help comes from the Lord, Who made heaven and earth.

PSALM 121:1–2 AMPC

Psalm 121 is labeled "a song of ascents," a type of hymn pilgrims sang as they made their way to Jerusalem. The first two verses are written in the first person, from the author's point of view. Perhaps the psalmist sang them to his fellow travelers as they climbed up the steps to the temple. As you read the words of Psalm 121:1–2, you can almost picture the speaker looking not at his feet but at his destination—the temple where the presence of God resided. For that is where his help lies.

The remainder of the psalm is written in the second person. The psalmist wants his fellow travelers—including *you*—to understand who God is and why they should seek Him for protection.

Dear woman and fellow traveler, know that God will not allow you to lose your footing. Nor will He sleep or doze off. Not only are His eyes on you, but He, your guardian, is "right at your side to protect you—shielding you from sunstroke, sheltering you from moonstroke" (Psalm 121:5–6 MSG). Thus, you can rest easy because your Lord "will keep you from all that is sinful. He will watch over your soul. The Lord will watch over your coming and going, now and forever" (Psalm 121:7–8 NLV).

Yes, life can be difficult, and the world can be quite

frightening at times. But it will grow even scarier if your eyes are looking to the ground and your feet are walking toward the wrong person, place, or thing for help and protection.

Today, if you're feeling helpless, stop for a moment. Consider where you may be looking for help. If need be, turn your eyes to look up, to those hills, to those heavens, to the place where the Lord is patiently waiting to give you aid, to deliver you, to lift you up to where He sits. Remind yourself that He will not let you trip up.

If you are frightened, not knowing how to stay safe from harm, look to your guardian, the almighty God. He is the one whose eyes never close, the one who protects you from the sun by day and the moon by night. He will not fail to keep you from all that might harm you—in this world and the next.

Each and every day, remember: "God guards you from every evil, he guards your very life. He guards you when you leave and when you return, he guards you now, he guards you always" (Psalm 121:7–8 MSG).

Thank You, my God, my guardian, for continually blessing me in so many ways. Keep Your eyes upon me, Lord. Help me look to You alone for help and protection. In Jesus' name, amen.

Learning to Listen, Wait, and Watch

Moses went back to God and said, "My Master, why are you treating this people so badly? And why did you ever send me? From the moment I came to Pharaoh to speak in your name, things have only gotten worse for this people. And rescue? Does this look like rescue to you?"

Exodus 5:22–23 MSG

You can just hear the frustration in Moses' voice. He'd had the idea that when God called him and Aaron to free His people, things would go smoothly. But instead they'd gone from bad to worse! Here's how things started. . .

Moses and Aaron arrived in Egypt and told the Israelites everything God had promised. Soon they would be free. "When they heard that the Lord had visited the people of Israel and that he had seen their affliction, they bowed their heads and worshiped" (Exodus 4:31 ESV).

Moses then saw Pharaoh and asked him to let God's people go so they could worship in the wilderness. But Pharaoh told Moses and Aaron to shove off. His slaves needed to get back to work. That same day, he made the people's work even harder, having them gather their *own* straw to make bricks *while continuing to meet their same quota*! This was proving to be quite a problem. As a result of their production shortage, the Hebrew foremen were beaten by their Egyptian bosses who asked, "Why have you not done all your task of making bricks today and yesterday, as in the past?" (Exodus 5:14 ESV). The bloodied foremen then complained to Moses and Aaron, asking why they'd come just to make things worse than before.

Moses, in turn, went to God. It seemed that both God (with His plan) and Pharaoh (with his cruelty) were only making things worse for the people of Israel. Yet Moses' question drew out what he needed: God's reassurance. For God told him, "Now you shall see what I will do to Pharaoh; for [compelled] by a strong hand he will [not only] let them go, but he will drive them out of his land with a strong hand" (Exodus 6:1 AMPC).

Perhaps you have asked God the same sort of question that Moses did. Why, when you were doing what He was asking you to do, did things get worse instead of better? Here is where you need to listen to God's answer, wait upon Him and His timing, and watch what He does next. Your victory, your freedom *will* come—just as it did for the Israelites. Your Lord *will* rescue you and others. And His rescue will be beyond what you ever hoped or imagined!

Lord, when doing Your will seems to make things worse than before, give me the patience I need to listen, wait, and watch what You will do next. In Jesus' name, amen.

The God with a Plan

"If you listen, listen obediently to how God tells you to live in his presence, obeying his commandments and keeping all his laws, then I won't strike you with all the diseases that I inflicted on the Egyptians; I am God your healer."

Exodus 15:26 MSG

God had sent Moses to His people to tell them His plan. First off, He wanted His people to know that He alone was their God. That He alone would free them from the oppression they had been suffering under the Egyptians—and that He would do so in a powerful way that would prove to them that He was their God. On top of that, He would bring them into the land He swore He'd give to Abraham, Isaac, and Jacob—because He was their God (Exodus 6:6–8).

Later, after getting His people out of Egypt with all kinds of treasure, parting the Red Sea, and wiping out Pharaoh and his chariots, God must have reveled in the praise and worship songs sent up to Him by His grateful people. But soon that praise turned to panic.

As Moses led the people into the wilderness, they went three days without finding water. When the thirsty travelers reached Marah, the water they found was so bitter they could not drink it. Those who just three days ago had been *praising* God began complaining to Moses. So Moses cried out to God, who then showed him a tree. Moses threw the tree into the water and the water turned sweet enough for the people to drink. It was there God made a deal with His wanderers: *"If you listen to Me and do what I tell you, things will go well with you."*

God has a plan for you. But not much will happen if you don't take the time to listen to what He wants to say or to do what He wants you to do. What you need to remember is that God plans good for you, not evil (Jeremiah 29:11). He wants you to believe that He will always provide for you. With God, your needs won't be met just once, but over and over again. That's where faith and trust come in. Because if you don't believe God will do what He says, nor trust Him to keep His word, if you're distracted by what's wrong in your life rather than focused on what's right, if you forget all He's done in the past and panic in the present, if you let the pressures in your life drown out God's voice, you'll soon find yourself walking circles in the wilderness instead of moving forward in the promised land. Which road would you rather walk?

Lord, You're the God with the plan. And I am a woman who desires to listen to Your voice and trust You to keep Your word. Let's head to that promised land together! Amen.

A Tried-and-True Remedy

Lean on, trust in, and be confident in the Lord with all your heart and mind and do not rely on your own insight or understanding. In all your ways know, recognize, and acknowledge Him, and He will direct and make straight and plain your paths. Be not wise in your own eyes; reverently fear and worship the Lord and turn [entirely] away from evil. It shall be health to your nerves and sinews, and marrow and moistening to your bones.

PROVERBS 3:5–8 AMPC

When you find yourself stressed, confused, uncertain, and under pressure, you may want to consider where you're placing your trust. Chances are you're leaning on your own understanding, knowledge, and perspective. Perhaps unknowingly, you've taken God out of the equation (stopped those heart-to-heart prayer sessions with Him and overlooked His advice, a.k.a. the Word). Because of seeing things from your own perspective instead of His perspective, you are likely walking down a crooked path, perhaps even losing your way. You've substituted God's all-knowing wisdom with your own very limited knowledge.

Proverbs 3:5–6 (NASB)—"Trust in the LORD with all your heart and do not lean on your own understanding. In all your ways acknowledge Him, and He will make your paths straight"—are words to be not only emblazoned on your mind and heart but repeated to yourself at least once a day. They are a vivid reminder that you *don't* know everything! They reinforce the fact that your own understanding is so much less dependable than God's that if you try to lean against it, you're bound to fall over!

When you begin to realize that all the things you want to fix are under God's wise, caring, loving, and thoughtful eyes and that He's the greatest handyman you'll ever know, you'll find it easier to breathe. Because suddenly, you realize you don't have to carry the whole world and its ills upon your shoulders. You were never built for that kind of responsibility anyway.

Make this day the first of many in which you trust in God with all your heart, leaving all your cares and concerns about the past, present, and future with Him. Realize that He can handle this moment in creation and all those to come. So ease up on that white-knuckled grip you're using, and just let go of everything. God's got this. God's got you.

Now you can breathe slowly, easily, calming your heart and your mind, refreshing your spirit and your soul.

Father God, forgive me for thinking I have more wisdom and understanding than You—the Lord of all creation. From here on out, I'm going to trust You, Lord, with all my heart, soul, and mind. I'm leaning on Your wisdom and listening for Your voice to tell me which way to go. In Jesus' name, amen.

God's Extraordinary Love

God shows and clearly proves His [own] love for us by the fact that while we were still sinners, Christ (the Messiah, the Anointed One) died for us.

ROMANS 5:8 AMPC

How much does God love you? He loves you so much that even while you were making mistakes, doing things He may not have approved of, and living a life away from Him, He allowed His Son, Jesus Christ, to die for you on a cross. Why? Because the only way God could bring you back into a relationship with Him was to have His Son die in your place. Wow. *That* is an amazing amount of love!

Jesus Christ, who died for you, loved you as well. How do you know that? Because His life was not *taken* from Him by others. Jesus *chose* to lay down His life (John 10:18)—so that you could live.

Yet that's not the end of the story of God's love for you. The wonder and the amazing beauty of it all is that nothing, "neither death nor life, nor angels nor principalities, nor things impending and threatening nor things to come, nor powers, nor height nor depth, nor anything else in all creation will be able to separate us from the love of God which is in Christ Jesus our Lord" (Romans 8:38–39 AMPC).

On those days when you feel unloved and unwanted by the world, think about what God and His Son did for you. Meditate on the fact that you have been loved by God from the very beginning and always will be. Consider what both God and Jesus sacrificed so you could live with them and the Spirit on earth and have a place reserved for you in their heavenly mansion.

If you *still* don't "feel the love," if you *still* aren't sure God loves or even likes you, dig into the Word. Meditate on the verses of love ringing out from Genesis to Revelation. You can start off with Jeremiah 31:3; John 3:16; 15:13; Psalms 86:15; 136:26; Deuteronomy 7:9; Ephesians 2:4–5; 1 Peter 5:6–7. Begin by reading the verse then writing it down. Read over the words once more; then close your eyes. Still your body. Focus on the rhythm of your breathing as first you breathe in and then out. Gently open your mind to the verse you've penned, trying to recall the words. If you need to read them over again, just slowly open your eyes once more. Then close them and lift up the words to God. Ask Him to unlock their meaning so that you can better understand them. Then ask Him to help you imprint these words of His love upon your heart.

Lord of love, thank You for loving me before I loved You. And continuing to love me day after day. In Jesus' name of love, I pray. Amen.

Write On

Write the vision and engrave it so plainly upon tablets that everyone who passes may [be able to] read [it easily and quickly] as he hastens by.
HABAKKUK 2:2 AMPC

Not only does God bless you with His Word, to which you have access every minute of the day, but He encourages you to *imprint* His Word upon your mind. But how do you go about doing that? By following God's tips.

God once told Jeremiah the prophet to write down His words (Jeremiah 30:2). God even encouraged His kings to copy out His Word: "When he sits on the throne of his nation, he should write this Law for himself in a book in front of the Levite religious leaders. It should be kept with him and he should read it all the days of his life. Then he will learn to fear the Lord his God, by being careful to obey all the words of these Laws" (Deuteronomy 17:18–19 NLV).

Why all this writing down of God's Word? So it will stick better in your mind. And when it sticks better in your mind, rather than relying on your own wisdom, you'll find yourself on God's page, following His ways, more often than not!

Although most people use the keyboard more than a pen and paper, studies have shown that writing things down by hand boosts your memory and helps you to better retain information and understand key concepts.

Writing down the needs of others can also ramp up your prayer power because you'll remember the names and requests better. And having stored up that info, chances are you'll also pray more often for those requests.

At the same time, writing down God's Word boosts your courage and strength. When the newly-returned-from-exile Israelites intended to rebuild Jerusalem's walls, they were threatened by the different peoples surrounding them. In order to keep the repair work going, the Israelites were forced to hold tools in one hand and swords in the other. To help the Israelites keep up their courage in this intense situation, Nehemiah told them, "Do not be afraid of the enemy; [earnestly] remember the Lord and imprint Him [on your minds], great and terrible, and [take from Him courage to] fight" (Nehemiah 4:14 AMPC). This method of imprinting may have been memorization of short and sweet verses that would give them a surge of strength and courage minute by minute.

God writes to you today, "Dear friend, do what I tell you; treasure my careful instructions. Do what I say and you'll live well. My teaching is as precious as your eyesight—guard it! Write it out on the back of your hands; etch it on the chambers of your heart" (Proverbs 7:1–3 MSG).

Lord, lead me into Your Word. Guide my hand and mind. Show me what words You would have me imprint upon my heart and write upon my mind today. In Jesus' name, amen.

God's Imprinting Service

This is the agreement (testament, covenant) that I will set up and conclude with them after those days, says the Lord: I will imprint My laws upon their hearts, and I will inscribe them on their minds (on their inmost thoughts and understanding).

Hebrews 10:16 AMPC

Just as God wants you to work hard at imprinting His Word on your heart and mind, God has His own imprinting business up and running, and all for *your* benefit! God so very much wants you to forever hold His Word within you that He has promised to imprint it upon your heart and inscribe it upon your mind! And with you helping God do such imprinting as you search God's Word and write down what speaks to your heart, you are bound to grow in your faith in so many ways as well as grow closer and closer to Him.

Not only will God help *you* imprint His Word upon your heart and mind, but He has done some *visual* imprinting of His own, saying, "I have indelibly imprinted (tattooed a picture of) you on the palm of each of My hands" (Isaiah 49:16 AMPC). Wow! That's how much God loves you! He's like a proud papa obsessed with keeping his child's picture right in front of him at all times!

Whether or not you think of God each day or remember His promises and how much He has done for you, you can be sure God thinks of *you* each day and remembers everything about you and what He has promised you. For about Him it is written, "He is [earnestly] mindful of His covenant and forever it is imprinted on His heart, the word which He commanded and established to a thousand generations" (Psalm 105:8 AMPC). The covenant referred to here is that of God leading His people into the land He promised them.

All that God commanded others to write down, all the words of His that begin at Genesis 1:1 and end in Revelation 22:21, were "written for our instruction, that by [our steadfast and patient] endurance and the encouragement [drawn] from the Scriptures we might hold fast to and cherish hope" (Romans 15:4 AMPC). What an awesome God we have, whose Word gives us direction, confidence, trust, hope, courage, peace, love, strength, and power. How wonderful that He will lead us to the word we need the most every day—and will use His hand to help our hand imprint His wisdom, lessons, and stories on our hearts and minds.

Lord, knowing You have my picture on the palm of Your hand is more than I can fathom. Thank You for keeping Your love and Word ever so close to my heart and mind. Amen.

Contentment, Clarity, and Calm

Praise the Lord, O my soul. And all that is within me, praise His holy name. Praise the Lord, O my soul.

Psalm 103:1–2 NLV

Today's challenges can sometimes be overwhelming. Some days it's easy to get carried along on the waves of discontent, confusion, and unrest in the world. Yet through the Word, you can find a way back to God and the contentment, clarity, and calm you crave. All you need to do is start praising God for the blessings that come from Him. Psalm 103 can give you a great head start.

First consider all the seemingly random acts of kindness God has bestowed upon you each day (verse 2). Meditate on how many times God has forgiven your mistakes, missteps, and sins and healed all your illnesses (verse 3). Contemplate how He has saved your life from eternal darkness and crowned you with loving-kindness and mercy (verse 4). Be more aware of how God fills your entire life with so many good things that you feel refreshed and renewed in body, spirit, and soul (verse 5).

Keep in mind each day that if and when people of power cause you to suffer, God is the one who will come in and perform what is right and fair for you (verse 6). He will even make His ways, acts, and methods known to you and share His plans with you (verse 7).

Continually remind yourself that your Lord is not an ogre but a kind Father who is filled with mercy and grace. He's not one to become easily angry, for He has an abundant and steady love for you (verse 8). He will neither nag, scold, hold grudges, nor give you the silent treatment forever (verse 9). And when you make missteps and mistakes, there is no way He will punish you as you deserve. Why? Because when it comes to you, His love and kindness are as big as the heavens are high (verses 10–11). He has removed your sins from you "as far as the east is from the west" (verse 12).

The point is God has done so much for you that you could spend the rest of your life writing Him a thank-You note. And these things He has done in the past, is doing in the present, and will do in the future for you are never ending.

To keep your head in the right place when the world is trying to pull you down into the wrong place, each day as you read God's Word, write down three ways God is blessing you. Then take a moment or two to thank Him, to revel in the light of knowing how much He cares for you. And the issues and problems of this world will fade away.

The ways You bless me, Lord, are beyond counting.
For that and so much more, I thank You. Amen.

Committing All to God

Roll your works upon the Lord [commit and trust them wholly to Him; He will cause your thoughts to become agreeable to His will, and] so shall your plans be established and succeed.

PROVERBS 16:3 AMPC

You had a plan. A surefire plan. It was a plan you were sure would succeed. So you took all the necessary steps, dotted all the *i*'s, crossed all the *t*'s, and have done everything that was in your power to do. Now you're anxiously waiting to see how things will turn out, praying and hoping for the expected success.

Yet that's not how God wants things to work. God wants you to commit to Him everything you think and do—to put all into His hands and not take anything back, nor be dismayed if things don't work out like you thought they would. Or be too proud when everything goes so much better than you hoped or imagined.

You may have had a plan, but God wants and ultimately has the last word to that plan (Proverbs 16:1). He will say if it's a good one or not, a go or a stop. He is the one who will make it effective, powerful, and successful—in His eyes.

Your mind may have planned the way you want things to go with your work. But God is the one who will direct your steps and show you how to carry out your plans, making them work perfectly for Him (Proverbs 16:9).

All these different verses from Proverbs 16 come down to one thing. God is in control of you and all you do. He is the one who will decide if something is a success. God shares these words of wisdom with you for a few reasons. These passages are a reminder that God is the one who is fully in control. That all you do in this life is in His hands. And here's the really good part, the wonderful, hidden blessing: Because God is in control, all the pressure is taken off you! You no longer have to worry about a project or plan being a success or failure. The outcome will be interesting, and you'll hope for the best. But when you've finished your work, you can breathe a sigh of relief and leave the outcome of your efforts in the hands of the one who created not just you but all that surrounds you—visible and invisible.

So today, dedicate whatever you do to God. Do your best with what you have and know; then leave the results in the care of Him who holds the entire world in His hands and knows what's best for it—and you.

What a relief, Lord, to know I can leave the results of what I do in Your hands! So I do that now, Lord, committing all to You. In Jesus' name, amen.

Sticking with God

"Blessed is the man who trusts me, God, the woman who sticks with God. They're like trees replanted in Eden, putting down roots near the rivers—never a worry through the hottest of summers, never dropping a leaf, serene and calm through droughts, bearing fresh fruit every season."

Jeremiah 17:7–8 msg

You know all the commercials that promise you so much that you highly doubt that the advertiser is legit? Well, this promise of God is not like that. For God means everything He has said in His Word.

If you can find a way to trust God with each and every thing that comes into your life and stick with Him through thick and thin, you too will become like a tree that has been replanted in the Garden of Eden. Your roots will go down into the earth, very near the water. No matter what happens in your day, your life, or your world, you won't give in to worry. You'll never drop a leaf. Instead of losing your composure, shedding all your fruit before it's ripe, melting from the heat, or freezing in the cold, you will be calm and filled with peace and bearing fresh fruit in season.

Because you trust in God, you know you'll be taken care of. You know your Lord and Master will look out for you, help you through every difficulty that comes your way. After all, He will have to because *you're* rooted to the spot you have in Him.

Perhaps you're wondering how you might become a tree like the one described in Jeremiah 17:7–8. A few clues are found in Psalm 1:2 (an echo of Jeremiah 17:7–8). There, the one who delights in God's Word, instructions, and teachings, the one who meditates on them and studies them, will become like one of these Jeremiah trees.

Why not put this idea to the test? Each day, leaf through God's Word. Study it; meditate on it. Imagine yourself relying on God no matter what happens, knowing that by living in His garden, you couldn't be in safer hands. Do this minute by minute, day after day, and you will find your worry has lessened to the point of being almost nonexistent.

Why waste your time worrying when you can have a much better and more peaceful existence by handing all your cares and woes over to God, sticking with Him through everything that comes your way, and leaving all insults, injuries, injustices, and influences in His hands. Get it into your head that God is on your side. And you'll have nothing to worry about.

Help me, Lord, to stick close to You in every season, drinking in Your Word and growing in Your way. In Jesus' name, amen.

Care Casting

Therefore humble yourselves [demote, lower yourselves in your own estimation] under the mighty hand of God, that in due time He may exalt you, casting the whole of your care [all your anxieties, all your worries, all your concerns, once and for all] on Him, for He cares for you affectionately and cares about you watchfully.

1 PETER 5:6–7 AMPC

Woman of the Way, God wants you to write something on your heart, to get it emblazoned on your mind. And that is. . .wait for it, because it's a biggie. . .God, the Lord of all, wants you to be content with the person you are. He doesn't want you to build yourself up in your own eyes and in the eyes of others. No, He wants that privilege for Himself.

So until God does lift you up just where and when He wants to, give Him all your cares and woes. Allow the weight of your worries to slide off your shoulders and onto His.

This idea of letting God carry your burdens is nothing new. David had the same instruction to each of his listeners in Psalm 55:22 (AMPC) when he told them to "cast your burden on the Lord [releasing the weight of it] and He will sustain you; He will never allow the [consistently] righteous to be moved (made to slip, fall, or fail)." David trusted his God. He knew God would hear his complaints when his heart was in anguish and when fear overwhelmed him. Things were so bad in David's situation that he wanted to have the wings of a dove and fly away. (Can you relate?) Yet he also knew that God heard his voice and would help him, just as God hears your voice and is more than ready and eager to help you.

If you have a problem, throw it onto God. Ask Him to carry all your worries—and *you* as well! You see, you were never made to worry about anything. You were created to be in a relationship with your Father. God wants to hear from you. And not just your praises but your petitions. He wants you to call on Him before you get so weighed down that you cannot rise up to Him in voice or prayer.

Today and every day, go to God with everything that's on your mind. Remember that He's interested in everything going on in your life. He doesn't just want to hear about your successes. He wants to hear about all your fears, worries, woes, and wanderings.

To You, Lord, I bring all the missteps, fears, slights, and worries that are keeping me from breathing easy in You. I'm casting all these things upon Your shoulders and leaving them there. In Jesus' name, amen.

Aaron's Blessing

And the Lord said to Moses, Say to Aaron and his sons, This is the way you shall bless the Israelites. Say to them, The Lord bless you and watch, guard, and keep you; the Lord make His face to shine upon and enlighten you and be gracious (kind, merciful, and giving favor) to you; the Lord lift up His [approving] countenance upon you and give you peace (tranquility of heart and life continually).

NUMBERS 6:22–26 AMPC

Aaron's blessing is one of the most powerful and well-known passages in the Bible.

Blessings are the way the priests invoked the power of the Lord on behalf of His people. And this blessing is a personal one, chock-full of all the ways God is promising to take care of each one of His people. That includes *you*.

The Lord has promised to bless you by bringing good into your life. That means God will give you success in your endeavors. He'll give you peace, loving relationships, and His very presence in your life. And He will always watch over you and guard you, keeping you safe.

God also says He will make His face shine upon you. That means He will notice you, be aware of you, and look upon you with favor. His sunshine-like presence and smiling face will beam down upon you from above, enlightening you and shining a light upon your path, helping you find your way.

God promises to be gracious to you. Not only will He be kind and loving toward you, but He will show you His mercy and favor. With approval He will look upon you, face-to-face, eye to eye. And as He does so, He will fill you with peace. The Hebrew word for peace, *shalom*, is used here. It means a true peace—harmony, wholeness, welfare, prosperity, and tranquility—and a continual peace throughout your life.

When you dig deep into these verses, you begin to realize how powerful and wonderful they are. To feel their full effect, read them slowly. Envision God performing each act of love and kindness upon you. Understand all He is offering to you and for you, minute by minute, hour by hour, day by day.

As the meaning of this powerful blessing sinks into your heart and mind, you will begin to actually experience this blessing from God, feeling its effects to your very core. And the bonus is that as this blessing becomes an integral part of your life, changing and reshaping you for God's good, you yourself will become a blessing to others.

Lord, thank You for keeping me, smiling upon me, walking with me, and changing my life of strife to one of peace. Amen.

A Mighty One in Your Midst

Fear not. . . . The Lord your God is in the midst of you, a Mighty One, a Savior [Who saves]! He will rejoice over you with joy; He will rest [in silent satisfaction] and in His love He will be silent and make no mention [of past sins, or even recall them]; He will exult over you with singing.

ZEPHANIAH 3:16–17 AMPC

Wondering where God is? Perhaps you are the one who has moved. For in His Word, God lets you know, repeatedly, that He is with you. That He is in your midst. And that He's not just any old god. No. *Your* God, the one "Whose power no foe can withstand" (Psalm 91:1 AMPC), is the Creator of all that is visible and invisible to your eye. He's the true mighty one who has saved you over and over again. He's your personal protector, warrior, and champion. He's your wall of protection, the barrier that shields you from evil.

Thus, there's no need for you to fear anything. Although you may sense danger coming your way at times, you can quiet yourself down by remembering that God is with you. If He is with you and for you, who can ever be against you (Romans 8:31)? So don't let any fears paralyze you or stand in the way of what God would have you do. Instead, work with confidence and energy in the assurance that the Lord God Almighty is with you with every breath you take, every step you make. You're as secure as a babe in arms with God by your side.

Not only is God your true and undefeatable defender, but this King of kings, Lord of love, and Savior of the world is ecstatic to be in and with you. So much so that He cannot help but rejoice over you! Truly, can you name anyone else who holds so much love for you and feels so much joy at just being with you?

And perhaps this is the best part, the greatest blessing of all: God has so much love for you, it is unutterable. Happy just being in your company, God remains silent as His heart bursts with adoration and joy. He won't be shaking His finger at you, giving you a hard time about bad choices you've made in the past. He won't bring up all the mistakes you've made, the missteps you've taken. There will be no I-told-you-so's. For all has been forgiven—even more, all has been forgotten. And there's another way your God demonstrates His love for you. Instead of recalling all the ways you've let Him, yourself, and others down, God will show His joy over you by breaking into song. What greater God do you need?

You, Lord, are so precious. And I'm so fortunate to be Your daughter. What joy and love we will share—from here into eternity. Amen.

Finding Calm in the Days of Adversity

The Lord knows the thoughts of man, that they are vain (empty and futile—only a breath). Blessed (happy, fortunate, to be envied) is the man whom You discipline and instruct, O Lord, and teach out of Your law, that You may give him power to keep himself calm in the days of adversity.

Psalm 94:11–13 AMPC

God knows our thoughts can lead us down the wrong path at times. Just when we think we have things figured out, God has a tendency to show how wrong we are.

Fortunately for us, we have both God *and* His Word. There we find His guidance, His teaching, His help. Within His scriptures—commands, laws, histories, poems, songs, letters, stories, and prophecies—we find our path, change our thoughts, and connect to God. With His wisdom planted deep within us, we can make better decisions. By reading about the missteps of His people, we know what pitfalls we need to avoid. But best of all, by listening to God's voice and then heeding His instructions, we find the power we need to keep ourselves calm amid adversity.

With God's teachings giving us strength to remain close to Him, unruffled no matter what comes our way, we can say we never would have made it through our conflicts and troubles—within and without—were it not for Him. The New American Standard Bible puts it this way: "If the Lord had not been my help, my soul would soon have dwelt in the abode of silence. If I should say, 'My foot has slipped,' Your lovingkindness, O Lord, will hold me up. When my anxious thoughts multiply within me, Your consolations delight my soul" (Psalm 94:17–19).

The ability to stay calm in troubled times is needed now more than ever before. Leaning into God's Word, keeping what He teaches you in the center of your heart and mind, you cannot help but find that beautiful peace that goes beyond understanding.

Today, go deep into God's Word. Make the Lord along with His scriptures your stronghold and rock of refuge. When uncertainty and troubles come knocking at your door, don't panic. Simply go to God in prayer, asking Him to lead you into His Word. There you will find the solace you seek and the peace He has promised.

May God give you the power to keep yourself calm in times of adversity.

Thank You, Lord, for knowing and then providing just what I need. Help me change up my thoughts so I can maintain my calm in mind, body, heart, soul, and spirit in these days. I will forever praise You, my rock of refuge and source of strength. Amen.

Jesus Never Lets You Down

The Master never lets us down. He'll stick by you and protect you from evil. Because of the Master, we have great confidence in you. We know you're doing everything we told you and will continue doing it. May the Master take you by the hand and lead you along the path of God's love and Christ's endurance.

2 THESSALONIANS 3:3–5 MSG

How wonderful to know that Jesus will never let you down. That no matter what happens in the world or in your circumstances, regardless of what comes your way, Christ will stick by you and protect you. You can be confident that's true because it's what God promises you in His Word, over and over again!

Yet that's not all! In God's eyes, you are a perpetual student, a youth continually looking for more and more wisdom so she can grow ever closer to Him. For there is always something new to learn about the Ancient of Days, always a new layer that He opens to you, allows to unfold so you can go deeper into and grow wiser about His will and way.

At the end of today's verses lies a blessing of which you can take hold. The apostle Paul prays that Jesus will take his readers (that includes *you*) by the hand and lead them along the path of God's love and Jesus' endurance as they wait for Him to return. How wonderful to hold that visual in your mind. Imagine Jesus coming along as you're reading this devotion, taking you by your hand, and leading you upon the path of God's love. Imagine that as you walk that path, you possess the patience to endure, the same patience that Christ showed when He was a man upon this earth.

At the very end of this letter, you will find two more blessings: "Now may the Lord of peace Himself grant you His peace (the peace of His kingdom) at all times and in all ways [under all circumstances and conditions, whatever comes]. The Lord [be] with you all" (2 Thessalonians 3:16 AMPC). The first invokes God's power to bring the peace of Christ to you. And not just when it seems easy or convenient, but at all times and in all ways—no matter what your circumstances! That is a major blessing, one you may want to speak out loud or meditate on every morning, before you begin your day's tasks. And the second blessing is even better. It calls down the presence of God to be with you—all. . .the. . .time. What a wonderful blessing to have upon you morning, noon, and night.

Dear Lord, I am blessed to have You beside me to protect me. Knowing You will never let me down keeps me calm in You. Amen.

Prayer: The Cure-All

Don't worry about anything; instead, pray about everything. Tell God what you need, and thank him for all he has done. Then you will experience God's peace, which exceeds anything we can understand. His peace will guard your hearts and minds as you live in Christ Jesus.

PHILIPPIANS 4:6–7 NLT

God has big plans for you in this life. He has a purpose for you that only you can live out. But you can't realize God's plans or live out your purpose if your head and heart are full of worry!

In his letter to the people of the Philippian church, the apostle Paul tells them not to fret. Not to have any anxiety or worry about *anything*. Instead, in every circumstance, they are strongly encouraged to go to God in prayer.

Prayer is God's gift to you. It's a way of communicating on a personal and intimate level with the God who actually created you! It's not that God doesn't know what's bothering you. But He does want you to come to Him with everything, every circumstance, every slight, mistake, concern, and worry, and leave it with Him. And He wants specifics! He wants to know who or what is upsetting you. When did it start? Where do you think the situation will go, or where might it lead you? How do you imagine things will turn out—and why? Your Lord and Master wants you to lay out all these ideas, thoughts, fears, and frets. He wants to know the particulars, where your imagination might be taking you, how you feel about it all, and what you want Him to help you with.

Before or after you bare your situation and soul, God also wants to hear you thank Him for what He has done for you, what He is now doing for you, and what He promises He will do for you. This process is to be repeated day after day—at the very least!

And why does God ask all this of you? Because He wants you to leave all your problems, cares, angst, and anxiety at His feet. For when you do, you will find the peace you require, the calm you crave, and the answer you need.

This peace that comes from sharing all with God is not just any peace. It's the kind that envelops your entire being. It banishes fear, soothes the soul, and softens the spirit. It gives you a peace that "exceeds anything we can understand. His peace will guard your hearts and minds as you live in Christ Jesus" (Philippians 4:7 NLT).

Lord, help me remember that I don't have to suffer from fear or anxiety. Instead, I can come to You and lay all that's on my heart and mind before You. In exchange, You give me the peace I so desperately need. In Jesus' name, amen.

Love and Forgiveness

For his unfailing love toward those who fear him is as great as the height of the heavens above the earth. He has removed our sins as far from us as the east is from the west. The Lord is like a father to his children, tender and compassionate to those who fear him.

Psalm 103:11–13 NLT

A double blessing from God—love *and* forgiveness!

God's presence and love are guaranteed to believers who are in worshipful awe of Him. The love He expresses to those who firmly and steadfastly follow Him is immeasurable. And because of and in honor of that love, God separates from us the blots on our records "as far as the east is from the west"!

It's God's compassionate love for us—the same love a good and honorable father extends to his own children—that moves Him to forgive us fallible human beings over and over again.

God understands who we are—dust particles in the wind. Job describes our lives like this: "We spring up like wildflowers in the desert and then wilt, transient as the shadow of a cloud" (Job 14:2 MSG). And Psalm 144:4 (ESV) says, "Man is like a breath; his days are like a passing shadow." Yet even though our earthly lives are short and sweet, God's love for us is forever.

The love and forgiveness God extends to us are a double blessing as well as an example of how we are to live our lives. Although we may not like to think about it every day, we know deep down that our lives on this earth are finite, our days numbered. Only God knows how long we will live on earth and when we will join Him in heaven. But as we live our days on earth, why not pass God's double blessing of love and forgiveness to those humans we love, our nearest and dearest? Perhaps that's part of our living wisely (Psalm 90:12), acknowledging our limited days on earth and making the best of the time granted to us by God's loving hand.

Ephesians 5:16 (ESV) implores believers to make "the best use of the time, because the days are evil." And in Jesus' eyes, the best use of our time is to love others as He has loved us (John 15:12) and to forgive others as He has forgiven us (Matthew 6:14).

Today, as you bask in God's double blessing of love and forgiveness, pass it on to someone you love. Do unto others as God has so graciously done unto you (Matthew 7:12).

Thank You, Lord, for the unconditional love and forgiveness You so graciously impart to me. Help me pass that blessing on to someone in my life today. In Jesus' name and power I pray, amen.

Persistent Faith

A blind beggar named Bartimaeus. . .began to cry out and say, "Jesus, Son of David, have mercy on me!" Many were sternly telling him to be quiet, but he kept crying out all the more.

MARK 10:46–48 NASB

In Mark 10:46–52 we read that Jesus and His disciples were on their way out of Jericho with a crowd of people following them. Sitting next to the road, the blind man Bartimaeus heard Jesus was passing by, so he yelled out for Jesus to have mercy on him. People told him to be quiet, but that only made Bartimaeus cry out louder.

Jesus stopped in His tracks and told His followers to call Bartimaeus over to Him. They did so, saying, "Take courage, stand up! He is calling for you" (Mark 10:49 NASB). So the blind man threw off his cloak, jumped up, and ran to Jesus' side.

Jesus asked him, "What do you want Me to do for you?" (Mark 10:51 NASB). Bartimaeus answered Him, saying he wanted to be able to see. "And Jesus said to him, 'Go; your faith has made you well.' Immediately he regained his sight and began following Him on the road" (Mark 10:52 NASB).

On the surface, this story looks like just one more instance of Jesus healing someone. Yet there is more to see beneath this simple account.

The first lesson is that persistence pays off. Bartimaeus could have remained silent when the people were trying to shush him. But he didn't. There was no way he was going to let Jesus pass by when he needed Him so desperately.

The second is that Bartimaeus didn't allow *anything* to encumber his sprint to Jesus' side. Whatever may have hindered him from getting to Jesus was tossed aside, bringing to mind Hebrews 12:1–2 (NASB): "Let us also lay aside every encumbrance and the sin which so easily entangles us, and let us run with endurance the race that is set before us, fixing our eyes on Jesus."

The third is Jesus so graciously asking Bartimaeus, "What do you want Me to do for you?" This is the same question Jesus asks all of us. When we pray to Him, telling Him what's wrong, Jesus wants a detailed account of what we want.

Lastly, Bartimaeus demonstrated his faith. He *knew* Jesus could heal him. There was no uncertainty in his request. That's why Jesus responded by telling him, "Go! Your faith has healed you" (Mark 10:52 NLV). This reply brings to mind the blessing Jesus reveals in the next chapter of Mark: "Whatever you ask for when you pray, have faith that you will receive it. Then you will get it" (11:24 NLV).

Lord Jesus, help me to be persistent, to allow nothing to stand between You and me, to tell You just what I want, and to have mountain-moving faith. Amen.

Contentment

I have learned how to be content (satisfied to the point where I am not disturbed or disquieted) in whatever state I am. I know how to be abased and live humbly in straitened circumstances, and I know also how to enjoy plenty and live in abundance. I have learned in any and all circumstances the secret of facing every situation, whether well-fed or going hungry, having a sufficiency and enough to spare or going without and being in want.

PHILIPPIANS 4:11–12 AMPC

The ability to be content no matter what's happening in your life, no matter what your circumstances are, may seem to be a major challenge these days. Yet the fact is, if you trust God to continually meet you where you are, how can you ever be *dis*content?

Couples often make tremendous sacrifices when they have small children and determine that one parent needs to stay home to attend to the young ones. In one particular family, the wife quit her job. Then one car was sold to save on insurance and vehicle maintenance costs. The husband took a part-time job in addition to his full-time employment. The young family watched others go on vacations as they sat in their backyard playing in a kiddie pool, year after year after year. Although their clothing was clean, it looked a bit more threadbare than that of other families. Yet the couple was quite content with less. They trusted God to meet their needs, and He came through for them time after time.

Later, when the children were of school age and the mother got a part-time job, the couple and their children were just as content with more. And when looking back at the leaner years, the parents realized some of their happiest days were when they had less than two nickels to rub together. Perhaps that was due in part to the fact that having fewer "extras" meant they spent less time taking care of them.

You too can be content no matter what your circumstances, no matter what situations may arise. That's *if* you believe "God will take care of everything you need, his generosity exceeding even yours in the glory that pours from Jesus" (Philippians 4:19–20 MSG).

How content are you these days? What things might you be able to let go of? How wonderful might it be not only to pare down your possessions but to realize the joy of giving freely to others?

Today, consider what you have. Thank God for it. Then ask Him if there's something He might want you to give away to help others in need.

Lord, You have already given me so much.
And for that I thank You. Now, what might You
want me to give to another in need? Amen.

For Such a Time

Do not flatter yourself that you shall escape in the king's palace any more than all the other Jews. For if you keep silent at this time, relief and deliverance shall arise for the Jews from elsewhere, but you and your father's house will perish. And who knows but that you have come to the kingdom for such a time as this and for this very occasion?

ESTHER 4:13–14 AMPC

An exiled Jew named Mordecai was raising Esther, his orphaned cousin, in Persia. When King Xerxes (a.k.a. Ahasuerus) was looking for a new queen, all the young virgins in the kingdom were brought to the palace and put into a harem. Eventually, Esther was selected by the king to become his queen. But as instructed by Mordecai, who was an attendant in the king's court, Esther never revealed to anyone the fact that she was a Jew.

The plot quickly thickens as the king promotes a man named Haman to be above all the palace officials. All the king's servants are to bow to Haman at the gate. But Mordecai refuses, determined to bow to no one but his God. Haman becomes incensed at Mordecai's rebellion, so he hatches a plot. Discovering Mordecai is a Jew, Haman tells the king that the Jews scattered through his kingdom are not following the king's laws. He then suggests that the king proclaim an edict whereby all Jews in the kingdom would be destroyed. The king agrees, and the edict is signed and sealed and delivered to all the provinces.

Hearing about the edict, Mordecai sends a message and a

copy of the king's decree to Esther, begging her to go to the king and plead for the lives of her people. Esther sends a message back to him, saying that if any person, including herself, goes to the king without being called, that person could be put to death. Mordecai tells her, "Who knows but that your position and purpose may be to do this very thing at such a time?"

In the end, Esther tells Mordecai to gather all the Jews in the city. They are to fast and pray for her for three days, just as she and her maids will do. Then she will go in to see the king. If she dies, she dies. As it turns out, Esther sees the king and lives. And later Haman loses his life while all the Jews regain theirs.

With your blessings comes a responsibility to use them to serve others when God calls you to do so. In so doing, you yourself, as well as your actions, become a blessing.

Ask God how you might use your blessings to bless others. And you just might find yourself doubly blessed!

Lord, I thank You and praise You for the ways You have blessed me. Please show me how I might be a blessing to others. In Jesus' name, amen.

Strength for All Things

I have strength for all things in Christ Who empowers me [I am ready for anything and equal to anything through Him Who infuses inner strength into me; I am self-sufficient in Christ's sufficiency].

PHILIPPIANS 4:13 AMPC

Life can be rough, presenting trial after trial after trial. Some people get so beaten down they can't get back up. But those who are Christ followers have a strength that is greater than that of mere mortals. They have the strength of Jesus Christ. Thus, no matter what the trouble or how often the trials, we need not sink or be counted out. Christ is in our corner, ready, willing, and able to help us not just get back up but win the battle!

Winning the battle can take many different forms. Sometimes, if the battle is temptation, the way to win is to exit stage left where Christ has opened a way for you to make good your escape. Or winning the battle may mean asking Christ to erase certain thoughts from your mind, thoughts that don't serve you, that lead you astray. Another option might be asking Christ to replace your thoughts with His own Word. A good start in that direction would be memorizing the words of Philippians 4:13.

Winning the battle may mean refusing to worry about things that may or may not happen to you. So much out there in the world plays on your fears, worries, and doubts. Of course, you definitely do need to be aware of and alert to certain dangers. But anything beyond that, anything that provokes you to mindless worry or needless fretting, you might need to compare to Christ and His power and strength, the same power and strength residing within you because *Jesus Christ* resides within you.

No matter what fix you may be in, no matter what trouble comes knocking on your door, no matter what trial may come your way, keep in mind that you are blessed because Jesus Christ has empowered you and strengthened you to do whatever needs to be done. The one who stopped the wind and calmed the waves can help you get through any storm that blows your way. The one who raised Lazarus from the dead can surely lift you out of whatever hole you may have gotten yourself into.

By living in union with Christ, you have within you all you need to stand up to this world's wiles and ways. With Jesus on your side, nothing and no one can stand against you or weaken your power.

Lord, with Your strength and power, I can do all things through You! Help me keep this truth close to my heart and mind so that I can do all You have called me to do. In Jesus' name, amen.

Practice Brings Blessings

Jesus got up from the supper and took off His coat. He picked up a cloth and put it around Him. Then He put water into a wash pan and began to wash the feet of His followers. He dried their feet with the cloth He had put around Himself.

JOHN 13:4–5 NLV

Imagine being one of the disciples. You've been walking with, listening to, and watching every move of this man above all men. You realize He's more than special: He's the actual Son of God. You've seen miracle after miracle performed. Now here you are, at a special dinner, the last He said He would be sharing with you. And you can't help wondering what the next days will bring.

Then your Lord gets up from the table. He takes off His coat and picks up a cloth. He's putting it around His waist. Next thing you know, He's kneeling down in front of you with a pot of water and begins to wash and then dry your feet! It's outrageous! But He's Jesus. And you've learned by this point to expect the unexpected.

When the Lord gets to Peter, a disagreement ensues. But soon all is sorted. Soon the Master rises once more, puts His coat back on, and then asks if you understand what just happened. He tells you that yes, He's your teacher and your Lord. And in saying that you're correctamundo. But He also wants you to know that just as in humility He washed your feet, you are to be humble and wash each other's feet.

That's just one more tidbit that Jesus has laid upon you and the rest of His followers. But this one has a blessing attached to it. For Jesus adds, "If you know these things, blessed and happy and to be envied are you if you practice them [if you act accordingly and really do them]" (John 13:17 AMPC).

Knowing that you, like your Master, are to be a servant to all is one thing. But actually serving others by doing what Jesus did is another. Yet there truly is a blessing in serving. But it's one you will never find unless you actually engage in service.

Foot washing is not for the faint of heart. For it does take courage and humility to kneel before someone, pick up her feet, put them in water, wash them with a cloth, and dry them with a towel. Performing acts of service for others—whatever they may be—allows us to feel the warmth of Christ's blessing as well as a strange sort of happiness.

Be a true servant of God and a follower of Christ. Don't just watch or read about what He would have you do. Actually do it. And you too will be blessed!

Lord Jesus, give me the courage, humility, and willingness to follow Your example in serving others. In Your name I pray, amen.

Jehoshaphat's Prayer: Eyes on God

Jehoshaphat stood in the assembly of Judah and Jerusalem in the house of the Lord before the new court and said. . . . We have no might to stand against this great company that is coming against us. We do not know what to do, but our eyes are upon You.

2 CHRONICLES 20:5–6, 12 AMPC

King Jehoshaphat was told massive enemy armies would soon be invading his kingdom. Although alarmed and frightened, Jehoshaphat didn't hide. He didn't try to solve the problem with his own wisdom. Nor did he sit down and cry. Instead, he decided to seriously seek God, and he asked everyone in Judah to fast.

So "Judah gathered together to ask help from the Lord. . .they came to seek the Lord [yearning for Him with all their desire]" (2 Chronicles 20:4 AMPC). Jehoshaphat stood among the people in God's house and admitted his army would not be able to fight the enemy knocking at their door. He admitted to God that he and his people had no idea what to do—but said their eyes were upon Him.

God responded to Jehoshaphat's prayer by speaking through Jahaziel, saying, "Be not afraid or dismayed. . .for the battle is not yours, but God's. Tomorrow go down to them. . . . You shall not need to fight in this battle; take your positions, stand still, and see the deliverance of the Lord [Who is] with you. . . . Fear not nor be dismayed. Tomorrow go out against them, for the

Lord is with you" (2 Chronicles 20:15–17 AMPC). Hearing these words, Jehoshaphat bowed with his face to the ground and worshipped God.

What a godly and humble king! Most leaders would not be strong enough to admit that they did not have the power to overcome an enemy. Nor perhaps would they bow down before God. But Jehoshaphat was a good and God-fearing king who knew where to go when desperate. And when he sought the Lord of all, humbly and faithfully, God responded in a mighty way.

You may not be a member of royalty or the commander of a country. But you can be humble enough to admit God is wiser than you. You can seriously set yourself to seek His wisdom instead of trying to solve problems on your own. And if you do, you will find God telling you what He told Jehoshaphat: *"Don't be afraid. I'm with you in this. I'll battle this one out for you. Just take your position, stand still, and watch what I do on your behalf!"* And then the only thing left for you to do is follow His directions and praise His name!

Lord, I have no clue what to do. But my eyes are on You. So here I am, seeking Your face, wisdom, and presence, knowing You'll take care of whatever comes against me. Amen.

Jehoshaphat's Miracle: Praise Above All

As they went out, Jehoshaphat stood and said, Hear me, O Judah, and you inhabitants of Jerusalem! Believe in the Lord your God and you shall be established; believe and remain steadfast to His prophets and you shall prosper. When he had consulted with the people, he appointed singers to sing to the Lord and praise Him in their holy [priestly] garments as they went out before the army.

2 CHRONICLES 20:20–21 AMPC

God loves to show His power among believers in amazing ways. And this second half of Jehoshaphat's story is a great example of that.

The morning after God told Jehoshaphat that *He* was going to fight this battle and that all Jehoshaphat and his people had to do was stand still and watch God deliver them, God's people got up early. Jehoshaphat told them to believe in God and in what He had said, and all would turn out well. Then, after conferring with his people, he chose *singers* to sing praises to God—*and sent them out in front of his army!*

As the people began to sing praise choruses of "Give thanks to the Lord, for His mercy and loving-kindness endure forever!" God began setting ambushes against the enemy armies. In the confusion, the enemy armies began fighting and destroying each other!

Some time later, when the people of Judah climbed the

watchtower that looked out onto the wilderness, they saw all the dead bodies on the battlefield—not one had escaped! All that was left was for Jehoshaphat and his people to take the spoil—cattle, goods, clothes, and other precious things. There was so much booty that the people needed three days to gather it all up! Four days later, they named the place of the battlefield the "Valley of Beracah [blessing]" (2 Chronicles 20:26 AMPC).

Jehoshaphat's story makes it clear that when you go to God, humble yourself before Him, seek Him with all your heart, trust Him with everything, and obey Him, all the while keeping your eyes upon Him, He will take amazing steps to answer your prayers. He will give you the confidence to raise your voice in praise while the enemy lies on your doorstep. And He will give you the victory you had never before imagined.

God has blessings just waiting for you. Are you ready to seek Him and allow Him to have His way in your life? If so, get ready! You're on your way to the valley of blessing!

Lord of all, help me to be humble before You. To seek Your help before anyone else's. To come to You with all my concerns, knowing You will find a way where I see no way. And help me, Lord, to obey You, knowing You will lead me to a valley filled with blessings! In Jesus' name, amen.

The Beauty of the Beatitudes: Part 1

When Jesus saw his ministry drawing huge crowds, he climbed a hillside. . . . Arriving at a quiet place, he sat down and taught his climbing companions.
MATTHEW 5:1–2 MSG

A book on blessings would not be complete without the Beatitudes. For a fresh perspective, we'll consider the way they are paraphrased in The Message. Before digging in, let's see how the word *blessed* in the "blessed are" statements is being used.

In this context, the word *blessed* is something more than a temporary feeling of happiness based on current circumstances. It goes much deeper. The Amplified Bible uses these words in parentheses to give its readers a more in-depth view of the meaning of *blessed*: "happy, to be envied, and spiritually prosperous—with life-joy and satisfaction in God's favor and salvation, regardless of their outward conditions" (Matthew 5:3 AMPC). In other words, it's that state a believer attains when she is in a good relationship with the Lord. It's a spiritual sense of overall well-being with God.

To begin, let's look at blessings 1–3.

Blessing 1: "You're blessed when you're at the end of your rope. With less of you there is more of God and his rule" (Matthew 5:3 MSG).

When you see yourself as depending on God to see you

through all things, then you will be blessed. To you, the Lord has become more important and yourself less important in every way.

Blessing 2: "You're blessed when you feel you've lost what is most dear to you. Only then can you be embraced by the One most dear to you" (Matthew 5:4 MSG).

When you've lost something or someone (financially, emotionally, or spiritually) because of a misstep or mistake, you'll seek out Jesus for comfort. And you'll find that He is dearer to you than anyone or anything.

Blessing 3: "You're blessed when you're content with just who you are—no more, no less. That's the moment you find yourselves proud owners of everything that can't be bought" (Matthew 5:5 MSG).

The English Standard Version Study Bible observes, "The meek are the 'gentle,' those who do not assert themselves over others in order to further their own agendas in their own strength, but who will nonetheless inherit the earth because they trust in God to direct the outcome of events."

Lord Jesus, help me be humble, content, and gentle, all of which will make me more and more like You. In Your name I pray, amen.

The Beauty of the Beatitudes: Part 2

When Jesus saw his ministry drawing huge crowds, he climbed a hillside. . . . Arriving at a quiet place, he sat down and taught his climbing companions.
MATTHEW 5:1–2 MSG

We've seen the blessings that come with being humble, content, and gentle. Let's take a look at the next three (numbers 4–6), remembering *blessed* means "happy, to be envied, and spiritually prosperous—with life-joy and satisfaction in God's favor and salvation, regardless of their outward conditions" (Matthew 5:7 AMPC).

Blessing 4: "You're blessed when you've worked up a good appetite for God. He's food and drink in the best meal you'll ever eat" (Matthew 5:6 MSG).

When we seek Jesus first and last in our day, when we can't live without Him spiritually, emotionally, mentally, or physically, when we long for an ongoing, right-standing, and faithful relationship with Him, we will know the gift of being completely satisfied by His presence—regardless of what's happening in our lives.

Blessing 5: "You're blessed when you care. At the moment of being 'care-full,' you find yourselves cared for" (Matthew 5:7 MSG).

When we truly *care* for others—and demonstrate that care, just as Jesus did—we ourselves will be cared for. When you show mercy (a sort of undeserved kindness) to others, others will show mercy to you. What a wonderful return on investment!

This beatitude is an echo of Micah 6:8 (MSG): "He's already made it plain how to live, what to do, what GOD is looking for in men and women. It's quite simple: Do what is fair and just to your neighbor, be compassionate and loyal in your love, and don't take yourself too seriously—take God seriously." It's walking as God wants you to walk.

Blessing 6: "You're blessed when you get your inside world—your mind and heart—put right. Then you can see God in the outside world" (Matthew 5:8 MSG).

When you are very close to Jesus, you will be truly *right* in your own heart and mind. It's then you'll see the purity around you and know God is working in your midst. You will begin catching glimpses of Him. As your spiritual eyesight develops, you'll start seeing Him more and more. With your eyes of faith, you will be able to see that God truly is good (Psalm 73:1). And if all that isn't enough, this blessing also promises that because of your purity of heart, one day you will see God in heaven.

It's amazing all the joy that springs forth when we seek to be as You would have us be. Help me do that, Lord, as I rededicate myself and my life to You, seeking to grow closer to You blessing by blessing. Amen.

The Beauty of the Beatitudes: Part 3

When Jesus saw his ministry drawing huge crowds, he climbed a hillside. . . . Arriving at a quiet place, he sat down and taught his climbing companions.
MATTHEW 5:1–2 MSG

We've seen the blessings that come with being humble, content, gentle, hungry, and thirsty to be right with the Lord, full of care for others, and right with God in our hearts and minds. Let's take a look at the last three, blessings 7–9.

Blessing 7: "You're blessed when you can show people how to cooperate instead of compete or fight. That's when you discover who you really are, and your place in God's family" (Matthew 5:9 MSG).

God wants you to discover the blessings that come with being a peacemaker. This blessing may remind you of when Judas brought a crowd of people to arrest Jesus. Moving to protect the Lord, one of His followers sliced off the right ear of a servant of the high priest. "But Jesus said, 'No more of this!' And he touched his ear and healed him" (Luke 22:51 ESV). When this incident is covered in John 18:10, Peter is the disciple named as the one who wielded the sword. In Luke we see how quickly Jesus moved to heal the servant. Jesus' peacemaking efforts precluded the mob from going after Peter. By standing between the two parties, Jesus prevented a potential disaster.

Blessing 8: "You're blessed when your commitment to

God provokes persecution. The persecution drives you even deeper into God's kingdom" (Matthew 5:10 MSG).

When you are hounded by others because you are standing firm in your faith but you refuse to back down, insisting on doing what Jesus would have you do or saying what He would have you say, you will find yourself ever closer to God and an inheritor of His eternal kingdom.

Blessing 9: "Not only that—count yourselves blessed every time people put you down or throw you out or speak lies about you to discredit me. What it means is that the truth is too close for comfort and they are uncomfortable. You can be glad when that happens—give a cheer, even!—for though they don't like it, I do! And all heaven applauds. And know that you are in good company. My prophets and witnesses have always gotten into this kind of trouble" (Matthew 5:11–12 MSG).

This last blessing is about following Jesus no matter what others say about you or do to you because of Him. But it's also about following all the beatitudes that came before, no matter who or what comes your way.

Lord, thank You for opening my eyes to what You would have me do and be to serve You and be truly blessed. Help me each day remember and take to heart at least one be-attitude as I live and grow in You. Amen.

Blessed Believers

Blessed (happy, to be envied) is she who believed that there would be a fulfillment of the things that were spoken to her from the Lord. And Mary said, My soul magnifies and extols the Lord, and my spirit rejoices in God my Savior. . . . For behold, from now on all generations [of all ages] will call me blessed!

LUKE 1:45–48 AMPC

Some blessings may not seem like blessings when you first receive them. . . .

Consider the young girl Mary. She was already engaged to Joseph and most likely very excited about her upcoming marriage. But one day, while she was minding her own business, an angel named Gabriel came to visit her. He said to her, "Hail, O favored one [endued with grace]! The Lord is with you! Blessed (favored of God) are you before all other women!" (Luke 1:28 AMPC).

Yet when Gabriel appeared, Mary didn't feel very blessed or favored. "She was greatly troubled and disturbed and confused at what he said and kept revolving in her mind what such a greeting might mean" (Luke 1:29 AMPC).

The angel obviously picked up on her emotions and confusion, for he responded by telling her not to be afraid. That she was favored by God. So favored that she was going to become pregnant, have a son, and name Him Jesus. He would become famous and be called the Son of God.

Mary was still confused, wondering how this was going to happen, especially since she was still untouched by a man.

Gabriel explained, "The Holy Spirit will come upon you, and the power of the Most High will overshadow you [like a shining cloud]; and so the holy (pure, sinless) Thing (Offspring) which shall be born of you will be called the Son of God" (Luke 1:35 AMPC). At the same time, he added that her cousin Elizabeth had conceived her first son in her old age. "For with God nothing is ever impossible and no word from God shall be without power or impossible of fulfillment" (Luke 1:37 AMPC).

Mary then said, "I'm God's servant. Let what you've said be done to me."

After the angel left, Mary went to see her cousin Elizabeth, who was six months pregnant. When Mary greeted her cousin, the babe in Elizabeth's womb leaped with joy! And she proclaimed a blessing upon the younger woman, whom she knew carried the Son of God!

Mary is a good model for women of the Way to follow. She believed the words of God sent by His angel. She trusted God to do the impossible. And no matter how her situation may have looked to others, Mary accepted not just the blessing but all the challenges that came with it.

Lord, help me willingly accept Your blessings,
no matter how impossible the fulfillment of them seems
or what challenges might come with them. Amen.

Blessed in Blessing

In everything I have pointed out to you [by example] that, by working diligently in this manner, we ought to assist the weak, being mindful of the words of the Lord Jesus, how He Himself said, It is more blessed (makes one happier and more to be envied) to give than to receive.

ACTS 20:35 AMPC

The Bible was written thousands of years ago. But the truth of its words is being proved more and more each day.

One ancient biblical statement that has been proven as true by modern studies is that it *is* better to give than to receive. Why? Well, first off, giving a gift of money or doing a random act of kindness makes us happy! Those feelings of happiness are reflected in our brains. The act of giving creates a "warm glow" effect. It may also release certain endorphins that produce a feeling known as "the helper's high."

According to another study, giving improves the health of people who have chronic illnesses and extends the life spans of the elderly. Some think this is because giving also helps to decrease stress!

Giving to others fosters cooperation and connections. "When you give, you're more likely to get back." Jesus already knew this when He told people, "Give, and it will be given to you. You will have more than enough. It can be pushed down and shaken together and it will still run over as it is given to you. The way you give to others is the way you will receive in return" (Luke 6:38 NLV). How cool is it that when you give to another person, you will be rewarded somewhere else down the line—and that reward may or may not come from the person you gave to!

Your giving induces feelings of gratitude—regardless of whether you're the giver or the receiver! And that feeling of gratitude is vital to your happiness, health, and social connections. Why not test this theory by keeping a gratitude journal? Every night write down three things you are grateful for or three good things that happened to you that day—no repeats! And see if it doesn't increase your happiness.

Lastly, your giving to others not only helps them but also has a ripple effect as it spurs others to give as well. How wonderful! It turns out that giving to others also releases a hormone called oxytocin. It "induces feelings of warmth, euphoria, and connection to others."[3]

For all those reasons—and because Jesus says so—make it a habit to give to others. And you will find yourself more blessed in your giving than in your receiving!

Lord Jesus, please show me who I can bless today! In Your name I pray. Amen.

Committed to God

The Lord *restored the fortunes of Job, when he had prayed for his friends. And the* Lord *gave Job twice as much as he had before.*

Job 42:10 esv

Job was a wealthy, good, and upright man who feared God and eschewed evil. He had a wife, seven sons, three daughters, and so many animals and servants that "this man was the greatest of all the people of the east" (Job 1:3 esv).

Things were going well for this good man. . .until Satan came before God. When God asked what he'd been doing, Satan said he'd just been cruising around, checking out what was happening on earth. God brought up how good, God-fearing, and wonderful Job was. Satan remarked that Job was good only because God had blessed him. As soon as all the things he had were taken away, Satan explained, he'd be sure to curse God. That's when God gave Satan permission to test Job. The only stipulation was that Satan could not hurt Job physically.

Next thing Job knew, his livestock were dead or stolen, his servants had been killed, and his children died when the house they were in collapsed. "Job arose and tore his robe and shaved his head, and he fell to the ground and worshiped. He said, 'Naked I came from my mother's womb, and naked I shall return there. The Lord gave and the Lord has taken away. Blessed be the name of the Lord' " (Job 1:20–21 nasb). Job never once blamed God for his misfortunes!

Back before God, Satan challenged God once more, saying that Job might have made it through those tragedies but would definitely curse God if, along with all those losses, he also lost his health. So God once more gave Satan permission to do what he would with Job—but not kill him. Thus, Job was stricken by Satan, leaving him with ulcers, scabs, and other sores from his head to his toes.

Job sat on a trash heap, using broken pottery to scrape his skin. His wife told him just to curse God and die already. But Job said, "Shall we indeed accept good from God and not accept adversity?" (Job 2:10 NASB).

No matter what happened to Job, through all the adversity he came up against, including bad advice from his four friends, he stayed committed to God. Not only did Job not curse God, but he grew even closer to Him, saying, "I had heard of You [only] by the hearing of the ear, but now my [spiritual] eye sees You" (Job 42:5 AMPC). In the end, Job was more blessed in the second half of his life than in the first.

Stay committed to God and obey Him through all things. And God will be sure to bless you for it.

No matter what comes today, Lord, help me stay close to and committed to You. In Jesus' name I pray. Amen.

Blessings Galore!

Blessed (happy, fortunate, to be envied) are all those who [earnestly] wait for Him, who expect and look and long for Him [for His victory, His favor, His love, His peace, His joy, and His matchless, unbroken companionship]!

ISAIAH 30:18 AMPC

God wants you to turn to Him, to settle down, to depend on Him for everything, to stop trying to save yourself. He puts it this way: "In returning [to Me] and resting [in Me] you shall be saved; in quietness and in [trusting] confidence shall be your strength" (Isaiah 30:15 AMPC).

As you then turn to Him, rest in Him, and quietly and confidently trust Him, waiting on Him and looking and longing for Him, God is doing His own waiting. Because He wants the best for you, He may have to delay your answer until He has everything all lined up: "He's waiting around to be gracious to you. He's gathering strength to show mercy to you. GOD takes the time to do everything right—everything. Those who wait around for him are the lucky ones" (Isaiah 30:18 MSG). Can you imagine God in heaven, clapping His hands in excitement, knowing you're going to love what He's preparing to come your way?

In the meantime, as you're waiting and God is lining things up for you, God is *eager* to hear you cry out to Him. He says He *will* answer your cry, your prayer, your knock as soon as He hears your voice, your plea, your beating on His door (Isaiah 30:19).

But what if you aren't sure you're where God wants you?

What if you think you've taken a wrong turn somewhere? What if you have come to a crossroads in your life and you're not sure which way to go? No worries. God has another blessing waiting for you!

When you are seeking Him but don't seem to be finding Him, when you're not even sure where God has gone from your life, cry to the Lord. When you do, "your Teacher will not hide Himself any more, but your eyes will constantly behold your Teacher. And your ears will hear a word behind you, saying, This is the way; walk in it, when you turn to the right hand and when you turn to the left" (Isaiah 30:20–21 AMPC).

You may not always be able to trust your senses or your thoughts or your emotions or your internal compass and timetable, but you can always trust your eternal Lord and Master—if you're willing to wait upon Him obediently and expectantly, with your eyes and ears wide open.

Here I am, Lord. I'm returning to You, ready to rest in You. Hear my cry. Tell me which way to go. Open my spiritual eyes and ears as I listen for Your voice and wait for Your presence to meet me. In Jesus' name, amen.

The Eyes Have It. . .or Not

When [Peter] perceived and felt the strong wind, he was frightened, and as he began to sink, he cried out, Lord, save me [from death]! Instantly Jesus reached out His hand and caught and held him.

MATTHEW 14:30–31 AMPC

Jesus had had a pretty busy day. It had started off on a rough note. Some people came to tell Him that His cousin, John the Baptist, had been beheaded. Hearing this news, Jesus went in a boat to a deserted place by Himself. But crowds of people heard about it and followed Him there. In sympathy, Jesus healed many.

Then, knowing the people were hungry, Jesus fed them—all five thousand men, plus all the women and children with them—after blessing only five loaves and two fish. As soon as the people had finished eating, Jesus told the disciples to get in their boat and head to the other side of the sea. He Himself went up the mountain to pray.

Some time later, the disciples were in the thick of a storm on the sea. As they struggled against the wind and waves, Jesus came walking toward them—on the water! This wasn't the way they expected to run into Jesus. At first, they thought He was a ghost. But when He told them to take courage, they knew it was Him.

Peter, bold as ever, blurted out, "Lord, if it is you, command me to come to you on the water" (Matthew 14:28 ESV). So Jesus said, "Come."

Peter got out of the boat and began walking on the water, heading toward Jesus. But when Peter took his eyes off the Lord and put them on the wind and the waves, he started to sink! So he cried out to Jesus, saying, "Lord, save me!"

Immediately, Jesus reached out for Peter, caught his hand, and held him. Then He said, "You have so little faith! Why did you doubt?" (Matthew 14:31 NLV).

What is your reaction when Jesus blesses you by commanding you to come to Him? Are you as eager as Peter, ready to jump out of the boat and, if you must, walk on water to reach His side? If you are ready, willing, and able—no matter what the danger—to follow Jesus, do you keep your eyes on Him? Or are you like Peter, suddenly seeing the strong winds and choppy waves that could sink you before you ever get to Jesus, and before you know it, you're underwater?

You're blessed to have a Savior who wants to be with you, hold you, calm you, save you, and encourage you. But to receive these blessings, you must keep your eyes on the one who can still the storms within and without.

Lord, my greatest desire and blessing is to be with You. Help me keep my eyes on You so I may safely and confidently reach Your side.

The Blessings of Knowing God

Acquaint now yourself with Him [agree with God and show yourself to be conformed to His will] and be at peace; by that [you shall prosper and great] good shall come to you.

Job 22:21 AMPC

The words above were spoken to Job by his "friend" Eliphaz. But because he spoke them to the wrong audience—the obedient and righteous Job—they were not true, at least not in that context. But there are higher truths within it that we may take to heart.

First off, we're to acquaint ourselves with the Lord. That means spending time with Him and in Him. It means looking into His Word and really getting to *know* Him, becoming familiar with His ways, wants, and wishes. We can also know God by seeing Him through the eyes, heart, and message of Jesus Christ. For He said, "No one knows the Son but the Father. No one knows the Father but the Son, and those to whom the Son wants to make the Father known" (Matthew 11:27 NLV).

That knowledge of God that we attain through our relationship with Jesus will give us the peace we so deeply want and need. That peace will free us from the storms brought upon us by our passions and cravings, our selfishness and tempers. No matter what changes come, we will find our anchor in the hope that good will come our way. Although we don't know from what corner or what cupboard we will find the unexpected blessing, we know it will come, for that is what God has promised us:

Genesis 50:20 (ESV): "As for you, you meant evil against me, but God meant it for good, to bring it about that many people should be kept alive."

Jeremiah 29:11 (ESV): "I know the plans I have for you, declares the LORD, plans for welfare and not for evil, to give you a future and a hope."

Romans 8:28 (ESV): "We know that for those who love God all things work together for good, for those who are called according to his purpose."

James 1:17 (ESV): "Every good gift and every perfect gift is from above, coming down from the Father of lights, with whom there is no variation or shadow due to change."

Each day, make a consistent effort to know God. Dig deep into His Word. Agree with what He says, even in those areas that make you uncomfortable. Conform to what He would have you do, say, think, and believe. Then you will find His peace and the blessings He is just waiting to pour upon you—on earth and in heaven.

Help me, Lord, to know You more and more, for in You and by following You, yielding to You, I will find all the blessings my body, soul, spirit, and mind crave. In Jesus' name, amen.

The Way Maker

Fear not, for I have redeemed you. . .I have called you by your name; you are Mine. When you pass through the waters, I will be with you, and through the rivers, they will not overwhelm you. When you walk through the fire, you will not be burned or scorched, nor will the flame kindle upon you. For I am the Lord your God, the Holy One of Israel, your Savior.

ISAIAH 43:1–3 AMPC

What amazing blessings are introduced to the reader of the Word through the verses above. The God who created you urges you to fear nothing. For He alone has saved you and has called you by your very name.

To God, you're not some faceless creature living upon earth for an undetermined amount of time. You're a certain woman with a specific name for whom God has a definite plan and purpose.

To help you live out your part in God's plan and perform His purpose for your life, God says He'll be with you as you pass through the waters, just as He was with the Israelites when Moses brought them out of Egypt and God held back the waters of the Red Sea so His people could walk on solid ground.

God will be with you just as He was with His people when they crossed over the Jordan. The priests worked together to carry the ark (God's presence) into the river and then stood stock-still as the waters piled up upstream. "And while all Israel passed over on dry ground, the priests who bore the ark of the covenant of the Lord stood firm on dry ground in the midst of the Jordan, until all the nation finished passing over" (Joshua 3:17 AMPC).

God will even be with you as you walk through fire, just as He was with Shadrach, Meshach, and Abednego. When those three friends were in the furnace, King Nebuchadnezzar said, "Behold, I see four men loose, walking in the midst of the fire, and they are not hurt! And the form of the fourth is like a son of the gods!" (Daniel 3:25 AMPC). When he ordered the men out of the flames, there was no hint of fire on their bodies, no singeing of their hair or clothes.

And why is God walking with you through flood and fire? Because you are precious in His sight. Because He loves you and would give men in exchange for you (Isaiah 43:4).

So do not fear. God is with you. This Lord who loves you will make "a way through the sea and a path through the mighty waters" (Isaiah 43:16 AMPC) and will deliver you from all harm.

Lord, the fact that You are with me through fire and rain, flood and flames makes my heart sing. Thank You, Lord, for always making a way where there seems to be no way. Amen.

A Matter of Talents

"Well done, good and faithful servant. You have been faithful over a little; I will set you over much. Enter into the joy of your master."
MATTHEW 25:21 ESV

To help His disciples understand the lessons they needed to learn before He departed from this earth, Jesus told many parables. One such story is the parable of the talents.

A man was leaving on a journey, so he called his servants to him and gave each a certain number of talents to invest. To the first servant, the man gave five talents. The next received two, and the last received one. Each one received a talent "in proportion to his own personal ability" (Matthew 25:15 AMPC).

To make "cents" of this story, it helps to know that in Jesus' day, six thousand denarii were equal to one talent. And a single denarius was the average payment for one day's worth of labor. Thus, one talent was equal to six thousand days (or sixteen years) of labor!

So what did the three servants do with their cache of cash? With his five talents, the first man made some trades and made five *more* talents. The second man traded with his two talents and made two talents more. The third man dug a hole in the ground and hid his talent.

When the master returned, he came to settle his accounts with his servants. The first man and the second man both showed the master how they'd doubled their money. To these faithful workers, he said, "Well done, good and faithful servant.

You have been faithful over a little; I will set you over much. Enter into the joy of your master."

The last servant cast aspersions onto his master, saying he was a harsh man who demanded the best. So, afraid of disappointing him, the servant had buried his talent. He then gave back what he'd been given originally: a single, solitary talent. Displeased, the master took the money from the play-it-safe servant and gave it to the servant who'd made the most. And the now talent-less servant was put out into the darkness.

God has blessed you with certain talents, resources, abilities, and opportunities, and He wants you to invest and use those gifts wisely. As you do so, He will reward you with even more "talents."

What talents has God gifted you? How are you using them for Him? Today, consider what changes you might want to make in using the talents with which God has blessed you. See where you might want to do some digging (or undigging), so you can do more investing.

Lord, help me faithfully and wisely use the talents, resources, abilities, and opportunities You have given me. In Jesus' name, amen.

The Blessing of Weakness

My grace (My favor and loving-kindness and mercy) is enough for you [sufficient against any danger and enables you to bear the trouble manfully]; for My strength and power are made perfect (fulfilled and completed) and show themselves most effective in [your] weakness. Therefore, I will all the more gladly glory in my weaknesses and infirmities, that the strength and power of Christ (the Messiah) may rest (yes, may pitch a tent over and dwell) upon me!

2 CORINTHIANS 12:9 AMPC

How often have you come down off a mountaintop experience and hit a valley so deep you had trouble climbing out? While in a deep valley, how many times have you bemoaned hardships, persecutions, illnesses, confusions, bad news, insults, and distresses that have come your way? How many times have you cried out to God with a tearstained face, asking Him to pull you up out of the pit, to make you less miserable, to just cut you a break?

The apostle Paul was given visions and revelations from God. But to keep the man humble, God also gave him a thorn in his side, a splinter in his flesh. At one point, Paul describes it as "a messenger of Satan, to rack and buffet and harass me, to keep me from being excessively exalted" (2 Corinthians 12:7 AMPC). Three times Paul prayed to the Lord, begging Him to rid him of this thorny splinter. That's when he heard Jesus say to him, "My strength, My power are completely fulfilled, are most effective in your weakness."

Now, instead of Paul begging for his thorn to be removed by God, he began to glory in it. For when Paul was weak, Christ's strength and power pitched a tent over him. This caused Paul to be pleased, almost cheerful when bad things happened. Now Paul no longer moaned, groaned, or complained about sickness, insults, confusion, persecutions, and distressing situations. All because Paul now understood that when he was weak in human strength, he was "strong (able, powerful in divine strength)" (2 Corinthians 12:10 AMPC).

Woman of the Way, when you're not strong enough, remember who is. The Son of God can move through your weakness, exhibiting His own light, power, and strength as He works through you to accomplish His own ends and purposes.

Think about the times you felt weak, when you had no strength to go on. . .yet somehow you did. That "somehow" was Christ working through you for His own divine purposes. How cool is that?

Thank You, Lord, for the hardships, illnesses, and issues I've experienced during which Your power worked through me. Help me remember, Lord, that the weaker I get, the more Your divine strength can shine through—all for Your glory! Amen.

Boundaryless Prayer

All the time that Peter was under heavy guard in the jailhouse, the church prayed for him most strenuously. . . . Suddenly there was an angel at his side and light flooding the room. The angel shook Peter and got him up: "Hurry!" The handcuffs fell off his wrists. The angel said, "Get dressed. Put on your shoes." Peter did it. Then, "Grab your coat and let's get out of here."

ACTS 12:5, 7–8 MSG

Prayer has no boundaries. It can go through walls, beyond nations, over continents, across seas, and into the heavens. It can exist throughout eternity.

Prayer is an extremely powerful tool in the hands of God's people. God says, "If My people who are called by My name put away their pride and pray, and look for My face, and turn from their sinful ways, then I will hear from heaven. I will forgive their sin, and will heal their land" (2 Chronicles 7:14 NLV).

Prayer is also easy to use. All it takes is your effort, your lifting yourself up to God. No actual words—thought or spoken—need be used. If all you can do is groan, God has you covered. He has arranged things so the Holy Spirit can do any necessary translation work (Romans 8:26).

Prayer can heal bodies, marriages, and hearts. It can give sight to the blind, hearing to the deaf, and water to the thirsty. That's why Paul was adamant that believers "be anxious for nothing, but in everything by prayer and supplication with thanksgiving let your requests be made known to God" (Philippians 4:6 NASB). He told the Thessalonians, "Rejoice always; pray without ceasing; in everything give thanks; for this is God's will for you in Christ Jesus" (1 Thessalonians 5:16–18 NASB).

Prayer was the first thing the new church turned to when the apostle Peter was arrested under Herod's orders. It must have kept the heavily guarded Peter calm, cool, and collected because he fell asleep while bound in chains and lying between two soldiers. The next thing Peter knew, an angel was waking him, his chains were falling off, and he was heading out the door.

Peter followed the angel out past the city gate, and then his heavenly helper disappeared. Peter then "came to himself" (Acts 12:11 ESV) and realized God had been behind it all!

Now free, Peter headed to Mark's house where believers were gathered in prayer for him. He knocked on the door, and a girl named Rhoda answered. Amazed that Peter was on the doorstep, she ran to tell the others, whose shock soon turned to joy when they saw Peter for themselves.

God has given you His blessing of prayer. Use it. Claim its power. And be amazed at the doors it will open.

*Thank You, Lord, for the gift, the power,
the privilege of prayer. For what or whom
would You have me pray today? Amen.*

Keepers of the Word

As he said these things, a woman in the crowd raised her voice and said to him, "Blessed is the womb that bore you, and the breasts at which you nursed!" But he said, "Blessed rather are those who hear the word of God and keep it!"

LUKE 11:27–28 ESV

Just as Mary had predicted in her Magnificat (Luke 1:48), people were calling her blessed!

A woman in the crowd, apparently overflowing with the wisdom she'd gleaned from the preaching and teachings of Jesus, shared her admiration of Him, saying that the woman who'd had the privilege of birthing Him must indeed be happily blessed.

Yet Jesus made it clear that those who hear God's Word and follow it to the letter are the ones who are *really* happily blessed. Why? Because God's Word gives them shelter in the storm, protection amid the flames, and wisdom along their path.

When you hear the Word preached, how do you keep hold of it? Do you pray beforehand, asking God to reveal what He would have you know and remember from the lesson you are taught? Do you jot down the scripture references and read them later? Do you write down whatever takeaways have touched your heart and meditate on them?

And what do you do when you are not in church but at home? Do you read your Bible every day—even if it's just one psalm, one proverb, one chapter, one verse? Do you mark up its pages? Do you ask God to shine His light upon what you read before you even open His Book? Do you meditate on what you've read, allowing it to guide you into God's presence? Do you pray God's Word back to Him? Do you memorize verses and ask God what they mean before you read any study notes? At the end of the day, do you go back to the Word, to your prayers, to your verses and see how they tied in with whatever you may have experienced that day?

Looking into God's Word, studying it, memorizing it, reflecting on it, saying it, praying it, as well as marking up your Bible or taking copious notes—all these things are great exercises for every woman of God. But do you know what is even more important? Living it. Obeying it. Following it. Using it to shine a light on your path. Making it an integral part of your life. *That's* what will give you the happiness and blessings for which your heart, soul, and spirit thirst.

Here I am, Lord, sitting before You. As I open Your Book, reveal to me what You would have me know, think, and do. Shine Your light upon Your words as I seek Your will for my life. Then, Lord, help me to keep the words You've highlighted. In Your name I pray, amen.

No Worries

Stop being perpetually uneasy (anxious and worried) about your life. . . . Look at the birds of the air; they neither sow nor reap nor gather into barns, and yet your heavenly Father keeps feeding them. Are you not worth much more than they?

MATTHEW 6:25–26 AMPC

Each and every day you have a choice: Either you can be anxious and worried about your life, or you can be calm and carefree. Jesus would like you to be the latter, not the former. That's why He gives you the words you can pray every day to keep yourself from fretfulness: "Give us this day our daily bread."

You need not say those exact words if you don't want to. You can say, "Keep us alive with three square meals" (Matthew 6:11 MSG), or "Give us the bread we need today" (NLV). The point is to ask God to give you what you need—every day. And then leave that request in God's hands, knowing and trusting He will provide for you.

Studies say that about 85 percent of the things you worry about *never even happen*! That's an amazing percentage. Can you imagine how much time you waste every time you wrinkle your brow or wring your hands? How about all those sleepless nights you could have spent resting easy instead of tossing and turning for eight hours? That's why Jesus commands you to "stop being perpetually uneasy"! Instead, take a look at the birds flying overhead. You can learn from them! Not only does God provide His feathered friends with food, but He also makes sure they get the water they need.

Have you ever seen a bird drink water? It bends down, slurps the water into its beak, and then tilts its head back so the water will cascade down its throat. When it does that, it almost seems as if it's looking up to heaven, thanking and praising God for every drop of water it imbibes.

The point Jesus makes here is that if God is providing for those birdies—which He loves, but not as much as you—imagine how much He's going to provide for you! Besides, worrying won't add anything to your life—not one inch to your stature nor one hour to your life span.

All Jesus asks you to do is to pray instead of worry. God knows what you need. And He'll provide that—and more—for you. But there is an *if*: *If* you "seek first the kingdom of God and his righteousness. . .all these things will be added to you" (Matthew 6:33 ESV). Sounds like a good deal. So why not take advantage of it? As you do, you'll find yourself a lot less worried and a lot more blessed.

Help me, Lord, not to worry about anything but instead to pray about everything. Amen.

Your Strength

I love You fervently and devotedly, O Lord, my Strength. The Lord is my Rock, my Fortress, and my Deliverer; my God, my keen and firm Strength in Whom I will trust and take refuge.

Psalm 18:1–2 AMPC

When you're in a tight spot, in major trouble, or as weak as a kitten physically, spiritually, mentally, or emotionally, God will supply the strength you require. What God did for David, the author of Psalm 18, God will do for you.

From the very first verse of this psalm, David tells God how much he loves Him, referring to Him as "my Strength." He realizes that calling upon God is the only way he'll be saved. As soon as a distressed David calls upon the Lord, the earth starts to shake. Fire comes out of God's nostrils. He speeds to David on the "wings of the wind" (Psalm 18:10 AMPC). God brings forth lightning, hailstones, fiery coals, and arrows. From His height in the heavens, God reaches down and pulls David up out of flooding waters. David, whose enemies are too strong for him, knows God can handle them.

Recognizing God's strength and ability to save him from anything is what gave David calm when facing calamity (Psalm 18:17–18). Because the all-powerful God was at his side, David could and did write, "By You I can run through a troop, and by my God I can leap over a wall" (Psalm 18:29 AMPC). Why? Because God girded him with the strength he needed (Psalm 18:32, 39).

David wasn't the only person who knew of God's strength.

Nahum wrote, "The LORD is good, a stronghold in the day of trouble, and He knows those who take refuge in Him" (1:7 NASB). Speaking through Isaiah, God said, "Fear not [there is nothing to fear], for I am with you; do not look around you in terror and be dismayed, for I am your God. I will strengthen and harden you to difficulties, yes, I will help you; yes" (Isaiah 41:10 AMPC). Speaking to God, Isaiah (12:2) declares that God is his salvation, strength, and song.

But Paul gives us the verse that helps us sink our teeth into God's strength. "I have strength for all things in Christ Who empowers me [I am ready for anything and equal to anything through Him Who infuses inner strength into me; I am self-sufficient in Christ's sufficiency]" (Philippians 4:13 AMPC).

Woman of God, you may have been told you are the weaker sex. But don't believe it. Although most men may be stronger physically, women have the upper hand in living longer, surviving sickness, bearing pain, and coping with heartache and trauma. More importantly, when you see God as your "stay and support" (Psalm 18:18 AMPC), who knows how much you'll accomplish!

Thank You, Lord, for being my strength. Into Your power I lean so I can do all You call me to do. In Jesus' name, amen.

Love Actually

Let everything you do be done in love (true love to God and man as inspired by God's love for us).
1 CORINTHIANS 16:14 AMPC

What's love got to do with it? Everything!

God wants you to do everything—not just one or two things, but *everything*—in love. Why? Perhaps because God is love. And the more love you spread, the more God you spread.

Yet you might be wondering exactly what love is. Perhaps it's time for a review of 1 Corinthians 13. At the beginning, we find that *love*—"that reasoning, intentional, spiritual devotion such as is inspired by God's love for and in us" (1 Corinthians 13:1 AMPC)—is better, much more valuable and important, than speaking in tongues, prophesying, having all knowledge, and having so much faith that you can move mountains. Even if you gave away all you had to the poor and gave up your very body, but didn't have love, you'd gain nothing.

Then the list gets down to the nitty-gritty, explaining what love actually is. It's patient, kind, not jealous, not boastful, not arrogant, does nothing wrong, never thinks of itself. Love doesn't get angry, doesn't cheer at wrongdoing, but is happy with all truth. "Love takes everything that comes without giving up. Love believes all things. Love hopes for all things. Love keeps on in all things. Love never comes to an end" (1 Corinthians 13:7–8 NLV).

To understand what love truly is, all you need to do is go back through that whole list. Wherever you see the word *love*, insert the name *God*. For your "God is love" (1 John 4:8 ESV). If you did that, the paragraph would then read like this:

God is patient, kind, not jealous, not boastful, not arrogant, does nothing wrong, never thinks of Himself. God doesn't get angry, doesn't cheer at wrongdoing, but is happy with all truth. God takes everything that comes without giving up. God believes all things. God hopes for all things. God keeps on in all things. God never comes to an end.

The premise we began with is a relatively easy one to remember—let everything you do be done in *God*—but living it out may be more challenging. Yet that's what we're supposed to do. Thank God we have His help to do what He dares us to do: to have, show, and mimic love in all we do and say. And as we do so, we'll be bringing more of His love into the world, now and forever.

Thank You for blessing me with Your love, Lord. Help me do everything in love. In Jesus' name, amen.

God's Masterpiece

"Are not two sparrows sold for a cent? And yet not one of them will fall to the ground apart from your Father. But the very hairs of your head are all numbered. So do not fear; you are more valuable than many sparrows."

MATTHEW 10:29–31 NASB

Did you know you are God's priceless masterpiece? It's true.

In Ephesians 2:10 (AMPC) we read that "we are God's [own] handiwork (His workmanship)." In other words, God made every little molecule, cell, and follicle that makes up your entire being—including your spirit and soul. He made your fingertips, colored your hair and eyes. Then, when His Son sacrificed His life for you and you accepted Him, God worked things out so that you would be "recreated in Christ Jesus, [born anew]" (2:10 AMPC). Thus you are the new and improved version of the original creation. But, you may be wondering, why would God go to all that trouble and sacrifice? That's another paragraph altogether.

God did all that for us so that "we may do those good works which God predestined (planned beforehand) for us [taking paths which He prepared ahead of time], that we should walk in them [living the good life which He prearranged and made ready for us to live]" (2:10 AMPC).

All those little details of your makeup are what make you so priceless. They are what make you more valuable to God than two sparrows. And the Word makes it clear that to God you are not just priceless but precious. That's why He has numbered all the hairs on your head—as well as your arms, your legs, your entire body!

One of the reasons God values you so much is because you, created in His image and by His very hand, are a reflection of Him (Genesis 1:27). God promises He will never forget you (Isaiah 49:15). Nor will He ever stop loving you (Jeremiah 31:3)! And His love for you is so great that even while you were still a sinner, living in rebellion against Him, He allowed His only Son, Christ Jesus, to die so that you could live (Romans 5:8). And He has made you His child (1 John 3:1)!

So here's the thing—what God really wants you to know, to engrave on your heart: Precious daughter, child of God, princess of the kingdom, sister to the Master, *you are loved and valued* by Father God far beyond what you'd ever hoped, dreamed, or imagined. So the next time you perceive yourself as of little value, send up a prayer to the one who sees you as His masterpiece. And He'll remind you that you're the invaluable and irreplaceable apple of His eye (Psalm 17:8; Zechariah 2:8; Deuteronomy 32:10).

Lord, thank You for making me an invaluable part of Your plan and purpose. Thank You that I am precious in Your eyes. Oh what love I hold for You, my beloved. In Jesus' name I pray, amen.

Christ's Hands and Feet

"I was hungry and you gave me food, I was thirsty and you gave me drink, I was a stranger and you welcomed me, I was naked and you clothed me, I was sick and you visited me, I was in prison and you came to me."

MATTHEW 25:35–36 ESV

Knowing the end was near, Jesus began making it even clearer to His disciples what He'd been trying to teach them all along, what they were to do in His name to show love, mercy, and kindness to others as they continued in their spiritual journey upon earth. He wanted to show them the proper spirit they would need on earth to outfit themselves for heaven.

Jesus wanted His followers to demonstrate acts of mercy by feeding those who were hungry and giving water to those who were thirsty. They were to invite and welcome into their homes the stranger, the foreigner, the one whose language, customs, skin color, and heritage differed from their own. Jesus wanted His disciples to clothe those who were naked and visit those who were sick or in prison.

By showing their compassion and commitment to being Jesus' hands and feet on earth, Jesus' followers would, in a time when they themselves would be facing persecution, be going that extra mile for others, regardless of the consequences, the risk of their own lives and well-being. Just as Jesus wanted His original followers to show love, mercy, and kindness on earth, He asks the same of you.

You are blessed to be an ambassador of Christ. To help

understand what that means, to get the idea firmly implanted within your heart and soul, look to this benediction from Saint Teresa of Avila:

> *Christ has no body but yours, no hands, no feet on earth but yours. Yours are the eyes with which he looks compassion on this world, yours are the feet with which he walks to do good, yours are the hands with which he blesses all the world. Yours are the hands, yours are the feet, yours are the eyes, you are his body. Christ has no body now but yours, no hands, no feet on earth but yours. Yours are the eyes with which he looks compassion on this world. Christ has no body now on earth but yours. Amen.*[4]

Today, realize the blessings you have in your own life. Then seek to find a way to serve those who need your love, mercy, and kindness on this side of heaven. Ask God where He would have you go, what He would have you do. And then be Christ's hands, feet, eyes, and body, full of compassion here and in heaven above.

Lord, I feel so blessed to be Your hands and feet. Who, what, when, where, and how would You have me serve? In Your name, amen.

Notes

1. Aly Semigran, "Experts Dish on Whether It's Healthy for Your Childhood Teddy Bear to Still Be Your VIP Bedmate," Well+Good, January 17, 2019, https://www.wellandgood.com/adults-sleeping-with-stuffed-animals/.
2. Semigran, "Experts Dish."
3. Jill Suttie and Jason Marsh, "Five Ways Giving Is Good for You," Greater Good Magazine, December 13, 2010, https://greatergood.berkeley.edu/article/item/5_ways_giving_is_good_for_you.
4. https://www.journeywithjesus.net/PoemsAndPrayers/Teresa_Of_Avila_Christ_Has_No_Body.shtml.